Programming Games for The ColecoVision and Adam

In Assembler

By Tony Cruise

Programming Games for the ColecoVision and Adam in Assembler

First published 2020, 2nd Edition 2024

Copyright © 2020-2024 Tony Cruise

All rights reserved

Special Thanks

Matt Householder - Editor,

Michael Thomasson – Forward & Cover Design,

The AtariAge Community

Table of Contents

Forward by Michael Thomasson 10

Preface 12

Acknowledgments 14

About this book 15

   Who should read this book? 15

   How this book is organized: A roadmap 15

   About the code 16

About the author 17

1.   Introduction 18

   1.1.   The ColecoVision 19

     Specifications 19

   1.2.   The Coleco Adam 20

     Specifications 20

2.   Getting Setup 21

   2.1.   Overview of the tools 21

     Emulators 21

     Advanced Text Editor 21

     Assembler 21

     Graphics Creation 21

   2.2.   Sprite & Tile Editor 22

   2.3.   Emulation 23

     BlueMSX 23

     OpenMSX 23

     CoolCV 24

     ColEm 24

     Gear Coleco 24

   2.4.   Editor/Assembler/Template 25

     Text Editors 25

     Assembler 26

     ColecoVision Assembler Templates 26

3.   The Structure of a Game 27

   3.1.   Setup/Initialisation 27

     Set graphics mode 27

     Initialise Sound Hardware 27

     Initialise Controllers 27

   3.2.   Title/Intro/High Score Screen(s) 28

Load Graphics and Patterns and Draw Screen(s)..28

Intro Screen Loop..28

3.3.   The Game Loop 29

Get Player Input, Move Player 30

Enemy spawn/initialisation...30

Move enemies...30

Collision detection 30

Animations 30

Draw changes to the screen..31

4.   Starting Z80 Assembler 32

4.1.   Memory and Registers 32

4.2.   Moving Things Around 34

4.3.   Let's Do Some Maths 35

Addition..35

Subtraction..35

Increasing and Decreasing 36

5.   Z80 Loops, Conditions and Bits 37

5.1.   Loops and Conditions...37

Jumps 38

5.2.   Bytes, Bits and Nibbles..40

What is Hexadecimal, You Say? 40

6.   Starting Somewhere 41

6.1.   Definitions..42

6.2.   Library Functions...45

6.3.   Main Source File..53

7.   Starting a Game 59

7.1.   Preparing the template..60

7.2.   Initialising our graphics 62

7.3.   Displaying Our Title Screen 63

7.4.   Displaying Our Game Screen...66

8.   Move and Shoot...69

8.1.   Moving the Player's Ship..69

8.2.   Firing a player bullet 71

8.3.   Move the Player Bullet..73

9.   Enemy Movement...74

9.1.   Step One – Asteroid Generation 74

Random Number Functions 74

Setup Code 75

Generate Enemies 76

9.2.   Step Two – Enemy Movement 79

9.3.   Summary 80

10.   Collision Detection 81

10.1.   Step One – Object Collisions 81

10.2.   Step Two – Enemy Collisions 83

11.   Scoring 84

11.1.   Displaying the Current Score 85

11.2.   Adding to the Current Score 87

11.3.   Subtracting from the Current Score 89

11.4.   Calling the Display Routine 90

11.5.   Adding Scoring to our Game 91

12.   Player Collisions and Lives 92

12.1.   Player Collisions 92

12.2.   Display the Player's Lives 94

12.3.   Game Over 96

13.   More Enemies 97

13.1.   Enemy Management 97

ROM Table 97

RAM Table 98

13.2.   Updated Code 99

Set up 99

Spawn Enemies 100

Move Enemies 102

14.   TMS9928A/TMS9929A - Graphics 105

14.1.   Video RAM Break Down 107

Graphics Modes I & II 107

Text Mode 109

Multicolour Mode 109

14.2.   Hardware Sprites 110

14.3.   Example Code – TMS Demo 111

Animating a tile pattern 112

Animating the colour table 113

More colour table animation 115

15.   TMS9928A/TMS9929A - Sprites 117

15.1.   Using Sprites 119

15.2.   On With Our Demo 120

Sprite shapes 120

Loading Sprite Patterns 121

Draw Our Sprites 121

Animate Our Sprites 123

Move Our Sprites 125

16.   Generating Sounds 127

16.1.   SN76489A Sound Chip 127

16.2.   Sound Example 129

17.   Sound Effects 131

17.1.   OS 7 BIOS Sound 132

Sounds Effects and Music Data 132

Sound Address Table 135

17.2.   Player Shooting 136

17.3.   Player Laser Hitting an Enemy 138

17.4.   Enemy Hitting Player 139

17.5.   Enemy Hitting the Ground 141

17.6.   Adding the Sound Effects to our Game 143

Adding Player Shooting Sound 143

Adding Enemy Object Destroyed Sound 144

Adding Player Ship Destroyed Sound 145

Adding Enemy Object Hitting Planet Surface Sound 146

18.   Playing Music 147

18.1.   Converting Notes to Frequencies 147

18.2.   Play a Tune 148

18.3.   Improving the Tune 151

18.4.   Adding the 2nd Track 153

18.5.   Stopping the Music 156

19.   Where to from here 157

19.1.   More Enemies 157

19.2.   More Complex Enemies 157

19.3.   Extra Lives 157

19.4.   Increased Difficulty 157

19.5.   Music 157

19.6.   Arcade Touches 157

Appendix A – ColecoVision BIOS Functions (OS 7) 158

Sound Routines 158

TURN_OFF_SOUND 158

SOUND_INIT 159

PLAY_IT 160

PLAY_SONGS 161

SOUND_MAN 162

Video Routines 163

FILL_VRAM 163

GAME_OPT 164

GET_VRAM 165

INIT_SPR_ORDER 166

INIT_TABLE 167

LOAD_ASCII 168

MODE_1 169

PUT_VRAM 170

READ_REGISTER 171

READ_VRAM 172

WRITE_REGISTER 173

WRITE_VRAM 174

WR_SPR_NM_TBL (EOS WR_SPR_ATTRIBUT) 175

Object Routines 176

ACTIVATE 177

CALC_OFFSET 178

GET_BKGRND 179

INIT_WRITER 180

PUTCOMPLEX 181

PUT_FRAME 182

PUT_MOBILE 183

PUTOBJ 184

PUTSEMI 185

PUTOSPRITE 186

PX_TO_PTRN_POS 187

SET_UP_WRITE 188

WRITER 189

Timer Routines 190

Timer Data Structures 190

FREE_SIGNAL 191

INIT_TIMER 192

REQUEST_SIGNAL 193

TEST_SIGNAL 194

TIME_MGR 195

Controller Routines 196

ARM_DBNCE 197

CONT_READ 198

CONTROLLER_INIT 199

CONTROLLER_SCAN 200

DECODER 201

FIRE_DBNCE 202

JOY_DBNCE 203

KBD_DBNCE 204

POLLER 205

UPDATE_SPINNER 206

Graphics Primitives 207

ENLARGE 208

REFLECT_HORZONTAL 209

REFLECT_VERTICAL 210

ROTATE_90 211

Miscellaneous Functions 212

ADD816 212

BOOT_UP 213

DECLSN 214

DECMSN 215

DISPLAY_LOGO 216

MSNTOLSN 217

POWER_UP 218

RAND_GEN 219

Appendix B – Adam Computer EOS 220

EOS Initialisation 220

EOS Memory Map 220

EOS Error Codes 221

EOS Functions 222

System Operations 222

Simple Device Operations 226

File Manager Operations 232

Device Driver Operations 238

Appendix C – Memory Map 242

Memory Maps 242

ColecoVision General Memory Map 242

Adam General Memory Map 242

Complete OS 7' RAM Map 243

Appendix D – Z80 I/O Ports Assignments 245

   ColecoVision Console 245

      Video Display Processor 245

      Sound Generator 245

      Game Controller 245

      Modem 245

      Expansion connector #2 245

      Memory Map 245

      Network reset 245

   Adam Computer 246

      Memory Bank Switch Port (7fh) 248

Appendix E – Distributing Your Title 250

   Standard Cartridges 250

   MegaCart 251

   High-Speed Tape 252

Appendix F – Text editor setup guide 253

   Setup Visual Studio Code 253

      Step 1 – Setting up the text editor 253

      Step 2 – Setting up the Z80 Assembler 253

   Setup ConTEXT 254

      Step 1 – Setting up the text editor 254

      Step 2 – Setting up the Z80 Assembler 254

      Step 3 – Add an execute key to ConTEXT for the Assembler 255

Appendix G – Opcode Games Super Game Module 258

   Memory Map 258

   Using the Super Code Module 258

References 261

   References 261

   Image Sources 261

Index 262

Forward by Michael Thomasson

I vividly remember receiving my very first videogame, *Cosmic Avenger*. It was a Christmas Eve gift from my grandparents. I thought for sure that an actual Colecovision console would emerge the following day. However, it was a big spend, well-above the family budget, and also the hard-to-find '82 Christmas item, so that didn't happen.

My mother advised me to return the *Cosmic Avenger* cart to the local department store and trade it for another toy, but I wouldn't hear of it, replying, "Someday I'm going to own a Colecovision!" Choosing to keep the title close to hand and heart, I read and re-read the *Cosmic Avenger* box and manual every day for an entire year. Finally, a Colecovision console materialized the following Christmas to much jubilation. It became "my first love."

My father fumbled with the TV box for what seemed like an eternity, but in time the Colecovision was properly connected to the telly. I marched Mario just past the first ladder when the picture blinked out, the result of a freak snowstorm that knocked the local grid offline. Eventually I had to go to bed, and as soon as my head hit the pillow, the power came back on, and I laid there listening to my older siblings play until I eventually fell asleep. It was the best gift my parents ever gave me, other than their love.

Fast forward over four decades later, and the Colecovision is still my "go-to" system that I continue to return to and play. If you are reading this book, after plunking down hard-earned cash to purchase it, you obviously loved the Colecovision just as much.

It is probable that, as a child, you also dreamed of designing your own games for your favorite home gaming system. I remember sitting at our family dinner table as a wee kid, with a stack of graph paper and a no. 2 pencil in hand, dreaming up ideas. I know that the author of this fine publication, Tony Cruise, certainly did. This book is proof of that... and so are his games!

Tony didn't just dream, he took action. He embraced the challenge and labored many long hours over countless nights, until finally his dedication paid off and he fulfilled his childhood passion. Even better, Tony is sharing what he learned with you.

In the 80's, video game programming was still in its infancy. Company secrets were well-guarded, documentation was poor, and without resources such as the internet, information was next to impossible to acquire. The fact is game programming for the Colecovision is much easier now than it was when Coleco was in its prime. It is even simpler with this book. That is reason to celebrate and, ultimately, only good news for you!

Homebrew support for the Colecovision has exploded over the last decade. In fact, new titles for the Colecovision more than double those officially released back in the day. The machine, and talented developers like Tony Cruise, continue to amaze, surprise, and impress.

Tony knows the Colecovision. He is arguably the best person in the world to write this particular book. In the mid-eighties, he started programming games for the Spectravideo SV-318 and SV-328 under the *Electric Adventures* label.

That may sound unrelated, except that the Spectravideo computers were MSX based. What is MSX, you ask? The abridged answer is that it is an initialism that is short for "MicroSoft eXtended Basic."

Without context, that doesn't mean a whole lot either. What MSX really tried to accomplish was to establish a single standard for home computing, similar to the VHS standard for video in the 80's, or the modern day digital optical disc data storage format known as Blu-ray. Basically, MSX was to unite computers so that software could be ported to multiple Zilog Z80-based platforms with ease instead of requiring a program for each system to be programmed from scratch, from the ground up, each and every time.

Tony programmed over fifty published titles for the MSX platform. Amazingly, the Colecovision was the only MSX-based video game console. This gave Tony a deep understanding of the console's inner-workings and eventually led to some of his *Electric Adventure* branded games to be ported to Coleco's console. He also programmed *Berzerk, Cavern Fighter,* and others for the Colecovision, and *Pyxidis, Block'em Sock'em, Kangaroo, Seaquest 99, Space Dungeon* are coming soon!

Writing MSX code in the 80's as well as in the modern day gives Tony a unique perspective that is unmatched by other Colecovision homebrewers.

Now read this book, and then read it again. Eventually, Tony's genius will start to sink in, and you will gain a firm grasp of understanding. Then dig in deep and start your own journey. We can't wait to play the new worlds that spring up from your mind and keyboard-typing fingertips!

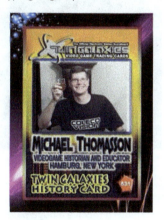

Michael Thomasson (GamerTag: ColecoCowboy)
President, Good Deal Game's Homebrew Heaven

Preface

I have been programming computers in Australia for over forty years.

Starting in the early 80s with the purchase of a 2nd hand TI-99/4 computer in partnership with my father, and then progressing to a Spectravideo SV-318 a year later, I loved playing games, mainly in the arcades and on the two main home consoles of the period, the Atari 2600 and Intellivision.

Having little money to spend on games, I decided to make my own versions for the Spectravideo.

Some early game listings were published in the local Australian user group publications and were received well at the time.

Then the entrepreneur in myself, thought, why not put some of these games on tapes and sell them locally and via the user groups. Thus the 'Program Pack' series of titles was launched with the initial pack containing one utility for drawing sprites, and three simple games.

This was soon followed by more and more titles and program packs, with over 50 games being released in a short period.

Figure 1 - Meteor Swarm (MSX/Spectravideo/Coleco)

After dabbling with enhancing some of the early games with add-on machine code routines, I decided to program my very first 100% machine code title, Meteor Swarm.

Heavily inspired by the arcade game Asteroids, this was very well received, and along with a cover designed by a local artist and a 2nd B-side title, Birds of Orion, was the very first release under the Electric Adventures name (the Program Packs were subsequently re-branded as Electric Adventures).

Around the same time, the ColecoVision was launched in Australia. Coming with Donkey Kong, as its pack-in game, the systems flew off the shelves.

I worked in the local games store that Christmas and can remember opening the store in the morning to receive a huge palette of ColecoVision systems, stacking them around the store and them being sold well before closing each day.

So, my first experience with the console was demonstrating the system in-store to customers and watching lots of lucky people take them home for Christmas.

My efforts, both working in the store and selling my titles paid off a few months later, with enough money to upgrade to a Spectravideo SVI-328 Mark II and most importantly an SVI-603 Colecovision adapter. Along with a ColecoVision joystick from a broken system, and several actual ColecoVision titles on cartridge.

Soon I was playing Mouse Trap, Q*bert, Frogger and Popeye at home and learning more about great games.

In the years that followed more, ever more complex machine code games were released (Munch Mania, Pyxidis and Video Grafitti), all of the titles were ported to the MSX systems after the purchase of an SVI-728, followed by a SVI-738 X'Press.

Next, I turned my hand to writing, starting tutorial articles on enhancing basic games with machine code (Beyond Basic), the Micro's Gazette magazine and finally the book 'Spectravideo and MSX Complete User Guide'.

Moving on from retail, I embarked on a career in the software industry, writing complex data-driven business applications; running a company, selling a market-leading Point of Sale solution; many years in the Financial Planning, Banking Industry, Tourism and Gaming, Resources and now the manufacturing sector.

In the last fifteen years, with a renewed interest in all things retro, I converted several of my titles from the Spectravideo/MSX originals across to the ColecoVision. As well as creating a video series on making retro games.

This series itself inspired the base content for this guide, which is all about the author's love of gaming and the want to share with fellow enthusiasts, the understanding of the steps and processes that go into creating games.

I truly hope this book allows more people to start making games for one of the very best 8-bit home consoles.

Tony Cruise

Acknowledgments

This book wouldn't exist without the support of my family, especially my loving wife and my four beautiful and talented girls who are themselves making their way in the world.

I would also like to thank the many friends I have met around the world with a passion for retro systems, for playing, collecting, or creating new games, and for seeing how far various systems can be pushed.

Thank you to Michael Thomasson for his wonderful forward, and for the generous editing support from Matt Householder.

About this book

Programming Games for the ColecoVision and Adam in Assembler is a comprehensive guide to developing your first retro game for the ColecoVision or Adam.

Throughout, all concepts are illustrated with a simple space-based shoot-em-up that is based on the awesome Astrosmash game reminiscent of games from your childhood.

Who should read this book?

For anyone interested in building their own retro games! No programming experience required.

How this book is organized: A roadmap

This book is divided into 19 chapters and 6 appendixes:

- Chapter 1: Introduction – An introduction to the ColecoVision console and the Adam Computer and what we will be aiming to achieve.
- Chapter 2: Getting Setup – We will go through the setup of various tools so that you can work towards creating new games for the ColecoVision and Adam, using your modern computer.
- Chapter 3: The Structure of a Game – How the structure of game is broken down.
- Chapter 4: Starting Z80 Assembler – We cover the basics of Z80 assembler.
- Chapter 5: Z80 Loops, Conditions and Bits – We cover a few more essential concepts in Z80 assembler.
- Chapter 6: Starting Somewhere – We with a simple demo ColecoVision project that provides the basic framework or template for making a game
- Chapter 7: Starting a Game – We start making our game, called "Mega Blast".
- Chapter 8: Move and Shoot – We get some objects moving on the screen.
- Chapter 9: Enemy Movement – We introduce some simple enemy movement.
- Chapter 10: Collision Detection – We add some simple collision detection so that the bullets our ship is firing can hit and destroy the asteroids that are falling down the screen.
- Chapter 11: Scoring – We add scoring to our game.
- Chapter 12: Player Collisions and Lives – We detect whether any enemy objects hit the player ship and display the number of lives the player has remaining.
- Chapter 13: More Enemies - We enhance the generation of the enemy objects.
- Chapter 14: TMS9928A/TMS9929A – Graphics – We cover some more technical details on how the graphics are handled on ColecoVision.
- Chapter 15: TMS9928A/TMS9929A – Sprites – In addition to the character tiles the TMS processor allows 32 sprites to be displayed on top of the background.
- Chapter 16: Generating Sounds – We look at how we generate sound.
- Chapter 17: Sound Effects – We use the OS 7 BIOS functions to add some sound effects to our game.
- Chapter 18: Playing Music – It's time to make our system sing, well play some simple music at least.
- Chapter 19: Where to from here – Our game is still quite simple and could do with several features added to turn it into a more polished and professional title.

- Appendix A: Colecovision BIOS Functions (OS 7) – This appendix contains information on the useful routines that are included in the ColecoVision's BIOS, also called OS 7.
- Appendix B: Adam Computer EOS - The Adam provides a set of additional BIOS functions called the 'Elementary Operating System' (EOS).
- Appendix C: Memory Map – The memory map of both the ColecoVision and the Adam computer.
- Appendix D: Z80 I/O Ports Assignments - These are the common I/O ports used by the ColecoVision and Adam Computer.
- Appendix E: Distributing Your Title – How to distribute your title to others.
- Appendix F: Text Editor Setup Guide – A more detailed guide on setting up the two featured text editors.
- Appendix G: Opcode Games Super Game Module – Make even more complex games using the hardware features added by the Super Game Module from Opcode Games.

About the code

The code for the examples included in this book is provided in a GitHub repository located here:

https://github.com/tony-cruise/ProgrammingGamesForTheColeco

The example code assumes the reader is using the TNIAsm or Glass assemblers mentioned in Chapter 2. Getting Setup. Instructions on setting this up are in section 2.4.

This book contains many examples of source code both in numbered listings and in line with normal text. In both cases, the source code is formatted in a `fixed-width font like this` to separate it from ordinary text. Sometimes code is also in **bold** to highlight code that has changed from previous steps in the chapter, such as when a new feature is added to an existing line of code.

About the author

Tony Cruise has worked in IT and application development for more than 40 years, starting with programming and releasing games for multiple 8-bit systems in the 1980s.

Author of more than 100 released titles, books, and magazine articles, today he is actively writing new games and utilities and creating resources for other developers working with 8 and 16-bit systems.

1. Introduction

This book aims to provide an overall guide on the steps required to start creating games for the ColecoVision 8-bit game console and its bigger cousin, the ColecoVision Adam Computer.

It will take you through each concept step-by-step, and rather than just being a technical guide, it will work through each stage with sample code and examples.

The code presented will focus on writing games using Z80 assembler, just like the developers of the original ColecoVision games used back in the day.

It is possible to use languages such as C or Pascal to make ColecoVision games, but that is beyond the scope of what is covered in this book.

In addition to the tutorial section, a full technical guide covering the BIOS built into the ColecoVision and Adam, and their respective memory and port maps is included.

Most BIOS calls include an example of usage or a reference to the tutorial section that covers it.

1.1. The ColecoVision

The ColecoVision console was released in August 1982, in North America, followed by Europe and Australia in July 1983.

Figure 2 - ColecoVision Console

In a market dominated by the Atari 2600 and Intellivision consoles, it provided the promise of arcade-quality graphics and game play, underpinned by having Donkey Kong as a pack-in game.

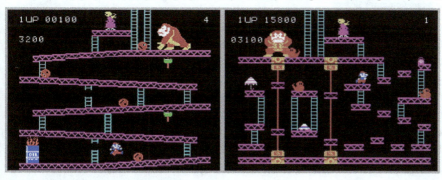

Figure 3 - Donkey Kong on the ColecoVision

A strong range of exciting, colourful arcade titles, along with licensed character titles like Cabbage Patch Kids and Smurfs, meant that retailers struggled to keep enough stock on shelves to satisfy initial demand.

The console's initial momentum was interrupted by the video game crash (mostly in North America) that dragged the whole home computer and console market around the world to its knees.

Today, the system's untapped potential, a strong user community, and the relative ease of making new and entertaining titles for the system have resulted in a growing selection of late-life, home-brew titles being released.

Specifications

Item	Specifications
CPU	Z80A 3.58MHz
RAM	1k
ROM	8k OS 7
Video	TMS9928A (NTSC)/TMS9929A (PAL)
Video RAM	16k

1.2. The Coleco Adam

In October 1983, Coleco released the Coleco Adam computer, both as a stand-alone unit and as an add-on module for users already owning a ColecoVision console.

Figure 4 - Coleco Adam Computer System

It was aimed at both the small-business and home-office user market, coming with a Daisy Wheel printer for high-quality (if noisy) printing, word processing and other productivity tools and high-speed storage with fast digital tape drives.

The Adam Computer was a serious investment ($US725) at the time, and initial shipments suffered from more than their fair share of faults, usually with the fast tape drives. This led sales to stall before they had a chance to gain much market share.

Users who persevered or joined the system later, when they were heavily discounted, ended with a robust, capable system that many would use practically for years to come.

Several add-on peripherals were released, and it has a strong owner community that has supported it to this day.

Specifications

The Adam Computers specifications are very similar to the ColecoVision, mainly adding a lot more RAM memory and the addition of the SmartWRITER inbuilt productivity software.

Item	Specifications
CPU	Z80A 3.58MHz
RAM	64k
ROM	8k OS 7 + 32k SmartWRITER/EOS
Video	TMS9928A (NTSC)/TMS9929A (PAL)
Video RAM	16k

2. Getting Setup

2.1. Overview of the tools

In the following chapters, we will go through the various tools needed so that you can work towards creating new games for the ColecoVision and Adam, using your modern computer.

The purists amongst you could use an Adam computer to carry out development, but this book is targeted towards the programmer working from a modern computer.

This method of using another, completely different computer to develop for another is called 'Cross Development' and involves using several modern tools to make it easier for you the programmer, to focus on creating your code and not be restricted by your development environment.

The tools we will go through include:

Emulators

These are programs that copy the functions of a ColecoVision or Adam in software running on another computer, they allow a very accurate representation of how your game will run on a real system.

We go into more detail in the next chapter on Emulation.

Advanced Text Editor

Back then, you were lucky to have an editor that allowed you to edit more than one line at once, let alone one that showed more than 40 columns of text and allowed you to navigate and search freely.

Luckily, we have lots of modern tools to choose from, for this guide I take you through a free editor called Text Editors

One of the most important tools needed to write assembly language is an application to edit the source files. This can be something as simple as Windows Notepad or Linux's VIM (or even ED for old-timers like me), but it is a lot better if the assembly text is formatted and coloured in such a way as to improve readability and highlight any potential syntax errors. It is even better if you can compile your current project and see any errors or warnings from the assembler.

Assembler

Assembly code commands are just text, but this is not the code that gets executed on the ColecoVision, for that we need a program that takes our text commands and turns them into the 'Machine Code' that the processor understands.

Graphics Creation

There are quite a few different tools available for helping with the creation of the background tiles and sprites you can use on the ColecoVision.

For this guide, I use my own tool, The MSX & Coleco Sprite and Tile Editor tool, that you can download for free from my website. We cover this in more detail in the next section below.

2.2. Sprite & Tile Editor

Sprite and Tile patterns can be made using a piece of graph paper, but it can be a lot of work, both making changes and then turning the pixels into the number values the ColecoVision will understand.

There are quite a few different tools available for manipulating graphics for the TMS graphics chip the ColecoVision uses, but I decided to write an 'all-in-one' tool for my use, that is easy to use and can save a lot of time creating and updating graphics.

It is called the "MSX/Coleco Sprite & Character Set Editor" and at the time of writing only supports the Windows operating system.

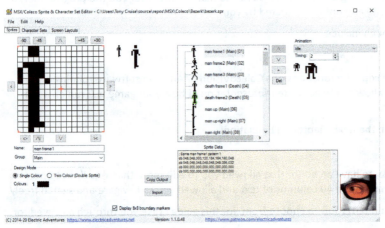

Figure 5 - MSX/Coleco Sprite & Character Set Editor

You can download the latest version here:

https://www.electricadventures.net/Pages/Article/108

2.3. Emulation

In the early 80s, development for both the ColecoVision and the Adam could have been carried out on an Adam computer, but other options exist in this modern age, with several good, software-based emulator programs that do an excellent job of simulating the original hardware.

In addition, these emulators provide more tools, such as an interactive debugger to see which part of our code is being executed and see the actual state of memory and Z80 registers.

The are several emulators available as follows:

BlueMSX

Supported Platforms: Windows Only

Website: http://bluemsx.msxblue.com

This emulator was created for the MSX range of computers but has had been extended over time to support several other platforms that use similar hardware, i.e. Z80 processor along with one of the TMS graphic chips.

BlueMSX includes profiles covering the ColecoVision, ColecoVision with a Super Game Module (SGM), and the ColecoVision Adam.

In addition, it has a good, easy-to-use, inbuilt, interactive debugger.

Being the one the author is most familiar with and the easiest to use (and get up and running for novice users), it is the main tool used in this book.

One thing to note, though, is that it has not been updated since 2013 and the Super Game Module (SGM) support is not quite accurate either and it has some issues.

OpenMSX

Supported Platforms: Windows, Mac OS, Linux, Android

Website: http://openmsx.org

The Open MSX emulator is an open-source platform that started around the same time as BlueMSX and was created as a cross-platform solution, primarily focused on MSX hardware.

It has continued to be updated in recent times and has had several emulation issues addressed.

It requires more technical knowledge to use i.e. primarily command-line based, with text-based configuration files. However, it does offer the user a large amount of flexibility and, of course, runs on just about any platform.

Support for the ColecoVision, along with both the Super Game Module and the MegaCart (see MegaCart) has been added in the last couple of years.

It does not have an inbuilt debugger, but being open source, there is a related project called Snapshot, that can be used.

There is also a graphical-based front-end available, as a separate project called Catapult.

CoolCV

Platforms: Windows, Mac OS, Raspberry Pi

Website: https://atariage.com/forums/topic/240800-coolcv-emulator-for-mac-os-x-linux-windows-and-raspberry/

CoolCV was created in 2015 by prolific MSX and ColecoVision (and Intellivision) coder known on AtariAge as Nanochess, who found himself holed up with a Mac laptop and a desire to run ColecoVision titles particularly some of the newer ones using both the Super Game Module and MegaCart.

It still has, as I am writing this, a sub-v1 version number, but I can attest to it being very stable and giving an accurate picture of how a title will perform on real hardware.

ColEm

Platforms: Windows, Linux, Android

Website: https://atariage.com/forums/topic/277355-colem-emulator-for-windows-android-and-linux/

Another emulator, specifically for the ColecoVision and Adam, that supports both the Super Game Module and MegaCart and is under active development.

It also supports the loading of Adam Disk and Digital Tape files and supports all Adam optional hardware, e.g. keyboard, printer, disk and tape drives.

Gear Coleco

Platforms: Windows, Linux, Mac OS

Website: https://github.com/drhelius/Gearcoleco

A much more recent emulator, that I have found to have extremely accurate sound emulation. It supports both the Super Game Module (SGM) and MegaCart ROMS.

Gear Coleco is a very accurate cross-platform ColecoVision emulator written in C++ that runs on Windows, macOS, Linux, BSD and RetroArch.

This is an open-source project with its ongoing development supported by backers, please see the web page for information on how to support the project.

It has an inbuilt debugger with a just-in-time disassembler, CPU breakpoints, memory access breakpoints, code navigation, debug symbols, memory editor, IO Inspector, and VRAM viewer including registers, tiles, sprites, and backgrounds.

2.4. Editor/Assembler/Template

In this section, we look at Text Editors, Z80 Assemblers and where to get the source code and templates for creating your own games.

I have included a code template for the ColecoVision system that will give you something to look at, compile and run in the emulator.

Next chapter we will be taking a closer look at Z80 assembler code, breaking down these templates and covering what they do.

Text Editors

One of the most important tools needed to write assembly language is an application to edit the source files. This can be something as simple as Windows Notepad or Linux's VIM (or even ED for old-timers like me), but it is a lot better if the assembly text is formatted and coloured in such a way as to improve readability and highlight any potential syntax errors. It is even better if you can compile your current project and see any errors or warnings from the assembler.

There are quite a few powerful and flexible text/code editors available. For this book we will focus on two: Visual Studio Code, available on Windows, Linux, and macOS and ConTEXT Text Editor, available on Windows. Some other well-supported text and code editors you could consider are:

- Notepad++
- UltraEdit
- Atom
- TextEdit
- Brackets
- CodePen

Visual Studio Code

Visual Studio Code is a powerful code editor that supports many different programming languages; has an extension framework; runs on Windows, macOS and Linux; and is free to use. To download and install Visual Studio Code, use the official site here: https://code.visualstudio.com/.

Platforms: Windows, Mac OS, Linux

Website: https://code.visualstudio.com/

There are several plugins available that support syntax highlighting and build command mapping for Z80 Assembler. One of the extensions to try is the extension called 'Z80 Macro-Assembler' by mborik. To find this in Visual Studio Code, go to the Extensions tab on the left-hand side and type "z80". The extension should be near the top of the list of items returned. Click it and click the Install button; you will need to accept and trust the publisher for the extension to be enabled.

For more information on getting Visual Studio Code setup see Appendix F -Setup Visual Studio Code.

ConTEXT Text Editor

Platforms: Windows

Website: http://www.contexteditor.org/

Z80 Syntax Mark-up file for ConTEXT (WLA-Z80 Assembler)

http://www.electricadventures.net/Content/LMARG/EP3/WLADXZ80Assembler.zip

For more information on getting ConTEXT setup see Appendix F - Setup ConTEXT.

Assembler

When writing your game code for the ColecoVision console, you will need to turn the text instructions that you type into actual machine code that the ColecoVision console will be able to understand. To do that, you need a program called an assembler.

A popular assembler used in the ColecoVision and MSX community for the Z80 processor is called TNIAsm.

The examples in this book have been tested with TNIAsm and an alternative call Glass, which although not as powerful runs on more platforms.

- Glass
    - **Website:** https://www.grauw.nl/projects/glass/
    - **Install Location:** c:\glass
- TNIAsm (version 0.45)
    - **Website:** https://www.electricadventures.net/Content/Downloads/tniasm045.zip
    - **Install Location:** c:\tniasm045

ColecoVision Assembler Templates

All the source files for this book can be downloaded from the Electric Adventures website here:

- https://www.electricadventures.net/Content/PGFTC/PGFTC-SupportFiles.zip

Or from the books GitHub support site here:

- https://github.com/tony-cruise/ProgrammingGamesForTheColeco

3. The Structure of a Game

The logic of a game can be broken down into the following high-level sections:

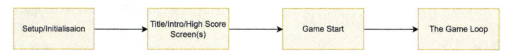

Figure 6 - The Structure of a Game

- Set up/Initialisation
- Title/Intro/High Score Screen(s)
- Game Start
- The Game Loop

3.1. Setup/Initialisation

At the start of the game code, you need to set up the ColecoVision (or Adam) ready for your game to run.

Set graphics mode

Before anything can happen on screen, the programmer needs to choose and select how to use the graphics display by selecting and configuring a graphics mode.

The ColecoVision has two main graphics modes, along with a text mode.

See TMS9928A/TMS9929A - Graphics for more details of the modes available.

Initialise Sound Hardware

Most games will want to play both sound effects and music. Both the sound hardware and the routines used to play sound effects and music need to be initialised.

See Sound Effects for an example of how to use the ColecoVision's sound hardware using the in-built BIOS sound routines.

Initialise Controllers

The ColecoVision includes BIOS routines for reading the various types of controllers that can be connected. To use them in your program the CONTROLLER_INIT BIOS function needs to be called.

3.2. Title/Intro/High Score Screen(s)

The next section of a game is the entry point for the players of the game.

This is where you tell them what the game is about, its title, what enemies you will be facing, and maybe some high scores to beat.

This could be:

- a single screen with a title image, waiting for the player to press 'Fire' on the joystick,
- or a collection of screens showing more information,
- or maybe even a demo mode showing the game in action.

Load Graphics and Patterns and Draw Screen(s)

First, we need to set up the graphical patterns that will be used to create our title screen(s).

We will cover this in more detail a bit later Displaying Our Title Screen.

Intro Screen Loop

Once the title screen has been displayed, a logic loop begins that could:

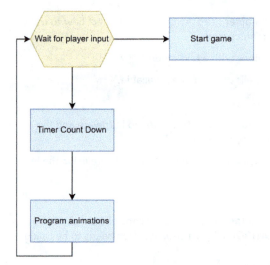
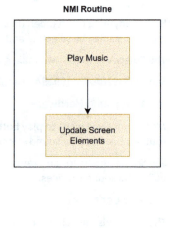

Figure 7 - Intro screen loop

- Wait for player input,
- Use a timer to count down to when the next screen should be displayed,
- Play music in the background.
- Animate part of the screen

3.3. The Game Loop

Next, is the most important part of a game, i.e. the main loop that controls the game logic.

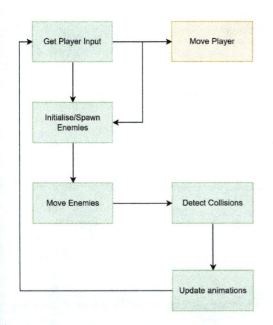

Figure 8 - The game loop

It can be split up into the following rough sections:

- Get Player Input, Move Player
- Initialise/Spawn Enemies
- Move Enemies
- Detect collisions.
- Animate
- Draw Changes to the Screen

Get Player Input, Move Player

This is where you get the players' input from the controller and then.

- move the player.
- shoot a bullet.

We cover this more in the chapter Move and Shoot.

Enemy spawn/initialisation

In this section, we decide whether new enemies should appear on screen and then set up appropriate information for controlling the enemy, e.g. place initial sprite(s), and set values in a RAM table.

We cover this more in the chapter Step One – Asteroid Generation.

Move enemies

In this section we move any existing enemies based on their current position and their state, using the sprite(s) and information in a RAM table.

An enemy might continue to move until it hits a boundary or might react on the player or the background.

We cover this more in the chapter Step Two – Enemy Movement.

Collision detection

Depending on the game, Collision Detection can be handled within the movement logic of the player and enemies, but also can be a separate step.

We cover this more in the chapter Collision Detection.

Animations

We also may want to animate the player's ship, enemies or the background, on a regular basis. Animation can make a game come alive, so is well worth including.

This can also be handled in both the player and enemy sections but can also include changes to the background.

Draw changes to the screen

Due to the TMS graphics chip having its own RAM (known as Video RAM or VRAM), separate from the Z80 CPU's RAM, changes to what is displayed on the screen must be sent to the VRAM so the TMS chip can display them.

Changes to the VRAM can only be done when the TMS graphics chip is not busy drawing the screen.

The screen is drawn, one row at a time, from left to right, until it reaches the bottom of the screen as follows:

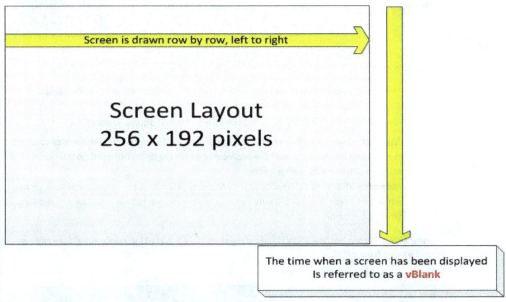

Screen is drawn row by row, left to right

Screen Layout
256 x 192 pixels

The time when a screen has been displayed
Is referred to as a vBlank

Figure 9 - TMS Graphics Chip - what is a vBlank

Once the bottom of the screen has been reached, the TMS chip raises a signal (the vBlank Interrupt) and then it needs to wait for the raster on the screen to return to the top for it to start drawing again.

This vBlank period is the time to change things in VRAM, while the TMS chip is not using it.

Trying to change VRAM at the wrong time can lead to incorrect output on the screen. It can be done, just with great care.

Note: The time to both read and write VRAM is longer while the screen is being drawn (as the TMS Chip is busy).

The signal from the TMS graphics chip causes a Non-Maskable-Interrupt (NMI) to be generated for the Z80 CPU.

The Z80 CPU will stop what it was doing and continue executing from the NMI interrupt address of 00038h.

It is the responsibility of the programmer to save any Z80 registers, used inside the NMI routine, and restore them before exiting.

Also, the programmer needs to signal the TMS graphics chip that the vBlank interrupt has been handled, so that it knows to send the next one when ready.

4. Starting Z80 Assembler

In this chapter, we cover the basics of Z80 assembler.

This will not be a full tutorial on Z80 assembler as that would require a whole book but should give you a start so you can follow on with the rest of this book, whilst doing some learning from suggested resources.

Now while we are on suggested resources, for Z80 there is no better than "Programming the Z80" by Rodney Zaks (ISBN: 0-89588-047-4).

Figure 10 - Programming the Z80

4.1. Memory and Registers

Programming is all about moving ones and zeroes from one location to another in the computer's memory.

The Z80 processor, like most processors, has two different ways to store information:

- **Registers** – These are the processor's internal memory locations used for doing calculations like addition and subtraction. They are located inside the processor itself, so they are the quickest place to access information.
- **Memory** – This is the external Read Only Memory (RAM) that the computer or console has, while a lot larger, it is located outside the processor. So, more time is required to read and write to a memory location.

Being an 8-bit processor, the Z80's standard registers store 8-bits of information, i.e. they can each hold a value from 0-255.

The names of the 8-bit registers are:

Register	Description
A	is also called the "accumulator". It is the primary register for arithmetic operations and accessing memory.
B	is commonly used as an 8-bit counter.
C	is used when you want to interface with hardware ports.
D	is not normally used in its 8-bit form. Instead, it is used in conjunction with E.
E	is again, not used in its 8-bit form.
F	is known as the flags. It is the one register you cannot modify directly.
H	is another register not normally used in 8-bit form.
L	is yet another register that is not normally used in 8-bit form.
I	is the interrupt vector register.
R	is the refresh register. Although it holds no specific purpose to the OS, it can be used to generate random numbers.
IXH	The higher (first) byte of the IX register. Note that 'I' is **not** the higher byte of IX. Combines with IXL to make the IX register.

IXL	The lower (second) byte of the IX register. When combined with IXH these two registers make up the IX register.
IYH	Again, this is the higher byte of the IY register. Note that IYH is different from both I and IXH. Combines with IYL to make the IY register.
IYL	The lower byte of the IY register. Combines with IYH to make the IY register.

Unlike some other 8-bit processors, the Z80 can also treat pairs of registers as a single 16-bit value which means, they can each hold a value from 0-65535:

Register	Description
AF	is not normally used because of the F, which is used to store flags.
BC	is used by instructions and code sections that operate on streams of bytes as a byte counter. Is also used as a 16-bit counter.
DE	holds the address of a memory location that is a destination.
HL	The general 16-bit register, its used pretty much everywhere you use 16-bit registers. Its most common uses are for 16-bit arithmetic and storing the addresses of stuff (strings, pictures, labels, etc.). Note that HL usually holds the source address while DE holds the destination address.
PC	The program counter. It holds the point in memory that the processor is executing code from. No instruction can change PC except by jumping to a different location in memory.
SP	The stack pointer. It holds the current address of the top of the stack.
IX	is an index register. Its use is like HL, but its use should be limited as it has other purposes and runs slower than HL.
IY	is another index register. It holds the location of the system flags and is used when you want to change a certain flag. For now, we won't do anything to it.

As you can see the Z80 has quite a lot of registers, all used for different things, which can get a little confusing.

The number of registers makes it easier to do certain tasks than other chips (like the 6502) with smaller instruction sets.

Still, you must know which registers you can use for different tasks. So, if unsure just check online or in the referenced book.

4.2. Moving Things Around

Hopefully, your head is not spinning too hard after studying the previous section and we can get onto the more practical parts of this chapter.

There is one instruction for moving something to and from memory or a register and it's called:

```
LD <target>, <source>
```

- <target> This is where the information will end up.
- <source> This is where the information comes from.

In general terms each of the <target> or <source> fields can be either a register, a memory location or an actual direct value.

If it is a register, then you just use the name of the register:

```
LD A,5
```

This will put the value 5 in the accumulator.

But you can also specify a memory location:

```
LD A, ($C000)
```

This will get the contents of the memory location C000h and put it in the accumulator.

If you want to calculate at a memory location, you can use some of the 16-bit registers:

```
LD HL,$C000
LD A, (HL)
```

The above two-line example does the same thing as the previous statement while giving us control of the memory location via the value in HL.

Most of the statements so far can work the other way around as follows:

```
LD ($C000),A
```

Save the value in the accumulator in the memory location C000h.

```
LD HL,$C000
LD (HL),A
```

Save the value in the accumulator in the memory location indicated by the HL register.

There are lots of combinations here and you can do quite a few of them with most of the registers, but not all. So, just check any of the online guides or the suggested book for more details.

4.3. Let's Do Some Maths

Now to round out this chapter, let's do something with some numbers and some basic maths.

Math operations with computer processors are based on addition, subtraction, and manipulation of bits.

For this quick look we will do some simple addition and subtraction to get you started.

Addition

To add two 8-bit numbers together we must use the accumulator as follows:

```
ADD A,<source>
```

<source> can be a direct value, another 8-bit register, or a memory location pointed to by HL.

```
; set up our values
LD A,5
LD HL,$C000
LD (HL),A
LD A,0
LD B,5

; now do our maths
ADD A,5
ADD A,B
ADD A,(HL)
```

So, in this example, each ADD statement would add 5 to the current value in the accumulator. At the end, it would contain a value of 15.

Now, if you want to do 16-bit maths, HL takes the part of the accumulator as follows:

```
LD HL,$C000
LD DE,$1000
ADD HL,DE
```

This would result in HL containing D000h.

Subtraction

To subtract one 8-bit number from another we must use the accumulator as follows:

```
SUB 5
SUB B
SUB (HL)
```

Notice there is no mention of the accumulator, as this statement only works on the accumulator. It is less typing but can be a bit confusing.

Now to do the same thing for 16 bits we have to use a different statement as follows:

```
LD HL,$C000
LD DE,$1000
OR A
SBC HL,DE
```

The instruction SBC stands for 'Subtract with Carry'. To make sure the Carry flag has not been set to 1 in a previous instruction, we add an extra statement, OR A, which will OR the value of the accumulator with itself to clear the carry flag.

This will result in HL containing B000h.

SBC can also be used with the accumulator for 8-bit maths where you want to include the carry flag set by something else (beyond the scope of this article).

Increasing and Decreasing

One more type of adding and subtracting is to increment or decrement a value by one. Now this could be done by just adding or subtracting the direct value 1 using the statements we have looked at above, but (to save both instruction space and increase speed) most processors have instructions to do this directly.

The Z80 versions work as follows:

```
INC <register>
INC (HL)
DEC <register>
DEC (HL)
```

So, these will increment or decrement either a single register (8 or 16-bit) or a memory location pointed to by HL.

Once again this is not supported by all registers.

5. Z80 Loops, Conditions and Bits

In this chapter, we are going to cover a few more essential concepts in Z80 assembler.

5.1. Loops and Conditions

Any programming language needs a way for different code to be executed depending on conditions.

Most processors have flags that signal a particular event has occurred after executing an instruction.

The Z80 gives us the following flags:

Flag	Description
S	Sign Flag. Indicates whether the accumulator ended up positive i.e. bit 7 of the accumulator is positive (0), or negative (1)
Z	Zero Flag. Indicates whether the accumulator is zero or not
H	Half Carry Flag. Is set when the least-significant nibble overflows
P/V	Parity/Overflow. Either holds the results of parity or overflow. Its value depends on the instruction used.
N	Add/Subtract. Determines what the last instruction used on the accumulator was. If it was added, the bit is reset (0). If it was subtracted, the bit is set (1)
C	Carry. Determines if there was an overflow or not. Note that it checks for unsigned values. The carry flag is also set if a subtraction results in a negative number.

These flags are stored in a special register called F (part of the 16-bit pair AF) that you don't access directly.

The flags are set when you execute any of the commands that affect the A register (or HL when doing 16-bit math's).

To check a value against what is stored in the A register, we use the CP (ComPare) command as follows:

```
CP 80
```

Executing this would set several of the flags depending on the value in the A register.

The CP instruction takes the value specified (or in the specified register) and subtracts it from the value currently in the A register. The contents of the A register is not harmed, but the flags are set as if you had performed a subtraction.

Jumps

Jumps in Z80 change the PC (program counter).

The jump can be a straight GOTO this memory location, but it can also include a condition based on a flag.

There are two types of jumps:

- Jump direct (JP)
- Jump relative (JR)

They are similar, especially when viewed from your assembly code, and each have a specific benefit. JR uses less memory, but the new address jumped to needs to be calculated, so takes more time to execute, whereas JP, uses more memory, but is quicker to execute.

With JR you can only jump 127 bytes forward or backwards. The best strategy is to use 'jump relative' in most instances, and only change it to 'jump direct' (or reorganise your code) when the assembler complains, or you need the speed improvement.

Now, adding a condition is simple, just add the name of the flag you want to test and a comma before the address.

For example, to jump relative if Not Zero you would use:

```
JR NZ, MYLABEL
```

MYLABEL represents another place in your assembly code. You could put in a physical memory address, but most of the time you don't need to worry about that. Let the assembler work them out.

To make this clearer, let's work through an example.

Say we wanted to do a specific task 10 times, we could do it as follows:

```
; set the number of times we want to go around the loop
LD B,10
; here is the start of our loop
; marked by a label, i.e. the spot we want to come back to
LOOP:
; This is where we would put the other things we want to
; do inside the loop
; Next we decrease or decrement our counter
DEC B
; This will set the (Z)ero flag if B reaches zero
; Now we do our jump with condition, i.e. if B is not zero loop
JR NZ, LOOP
```

If the code inside this loop ends up being larger than 127 bytes, the assembler will tell you by generating an error. You only need to change the 'JR' to 'JP' and it will fix the issue.

Now, there is a better way of doing this loop in Z80, and with Z80 you will find there are often several ways of doing the same thing.

For the level of code we will be writing, it doesn't really matter which looping method you use. The most important thing is to make sure that you can understand what has been coded when you come back to it later.

But for the curious, Z80 has a rather helpful instruction called DJNZ, which stands for Decrement and Jump when **N**on-**Z**ero.

It only works with the B register and the jump is relative, so you need to keep that in mind.

So, the same example would work as follows:

```
; set the number of times we want to go around the loop
LD B,10
; mark the start of the loop
LOOP:
; This is where we put the other contents of the loop
; Now we decrement and jump when non-zero
DJNZ LOOP
```

As you can see, it loops with less code. It makes things simpler and as a side benefit it is both easier to read and faster.

5.2.Bytes, Bits and Nibbles

We are almost done covering the Basics of Z80 programming; it's a good idea to cover Bits as our game will use pixels, which are represented by one or more bits stored in our system's memory.

A single location in memory contains a Byte, which is made up of 8 bits as follows:

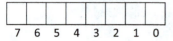

This allows each Byte to contain a number from 0 to 255. We make larger numbers by combining bytes together (a topic for another time).

One more term to know is that the two halves of a Byte (Bits 0-3 and 4-7) are known as Nibbles and each Nibble represents a number from 0-15 or 0-F in hexadecimal.

What is Hexadecimal, You Say?

Humans have ten fingers and ten toes. So, it is little wonder that we count things by breaking them down into groups of ten, but all computers know about are 1's and 0's, which means computer numbers are broken down into powers of 2.

Hexadecimal is a way of easily expressing the numbers from 0-15 with one character as follows:

Decimal	Hexadecimal	Decimal	Hexadecimal
0	0	8	8
1	1	9	9
2	2	10	A
3	3	11	B
4	4	12	C
5	5	13	D
6	6	14	E
7	7	15	F

So, a single Hexadecimal digit represents one Nibble and, thus, you only need two characters to represent a Byte of computer memory. Therefore, Hexadecimal is very convenient when writing assembly code.

Hopefully, these last two chapters have given you a start on understanding programming in assembly language. Next, we start making a program to run on a ColecoVision console.

6. Starting Somewhere

We are going to create a simple space shooting game throughout the rest of the tutorial, but before we get too carried away, we should start with a simpler demo ColecoVision project that provides the basic framework or template for making a game.

This demo does all the required setup to get the machine up and running, placing some text on the screen and two objects.

- a ball that bounces around the screen and
- a bat that is moved via the joystick controller.

This is a fair bit of code, but like the other chapters, you can either type it in from this book or download it from the supporting website.

The source code is split into three files as follows:

- Definitions
- Library Functions
- Main Source File

Once again, this is a lot of code (and text) in the book, with little explanation, other than code comments, so feel free to jump to the next chapter.

It is included here for completeness, as a printed book lasts for the life of its paper, whereas a web site is only valid if it is still hosted.

6.1. Definitions

The Definitions or Include file, as it is often called, contains the calling locations of the ColecoVision BIOS routines that can be called, and useful named values.

```
;------------------------------------------------
; Coleco ver 1.02 (C) Electric Adventures 2020
;------------------------------------------------
;
; Coleco Ports
;
; Video Display Processor
DATA_PORT: EQU 0beh
CTRL_PORT: EQU 0bfh
;
; Sound Generator
SND_PORT:  EQU 0ffh ; write only
;
; Game Controller
GC_STROBE_SET:   EQU 080h ; write only
GC_STROBE_RESET: EQU 0c0h ; write only
GC_CONTROLLER1:  EQU 0fch ; read only
GC_CONTROLLER2:  EQU 0ffh ; read only
;
; Video modes
SCRMODE_STANDARD:                 EQU 00h
SCRMODE_TEXT:                     EQU 10h
SCRMODE_MULTICOLOR:               EQU 08h
SCRMODE_BITMAP:                   EQU 02h
SCRMODE_BITMAP_TEXT:              EQU 12h
SCRMODE_BITMAP_MULTICOLOR:        EQU 0ah
SCRMODE_BITMAP_TEXT_MULTICOLOR:   EQU 1ah
;
; TMS99xxA colours
COLOR_TRANSPARENT:     EQU 00h
COLOR_BLACK:           EQU 01h
COLOR_GREEN:           EQU 02h
COLOR_LIGHT_GREEN:     EQU 03h
COLOR_BLUE:            EQU 04h
COLOR_LIGHT_BLUE:      EQU 05h
COLOR_DARK_RED:        EQU 06h
COLOR_CYAN:            EQU 07h
COLOR_RED:             EQU 08h
COLOR_LIGHT_RED:       EQU 09h
COLOR_YELLOW:          EQU 0ah
COLOR_LIGHT_YELLOW:    EQU 0bh
COLOR_DARK_GREEN:      EQU 0ch
COLOR_MAGENTA:         EQU 0dh
COLOR_GRAY:            EQU 0eh
COLOR_WHITE:           EQU 0fh
;
; Coleco BIOS Jump Table
;
; Misc calls
ADD816:        EQU $01b1        ; Add 8-bit value to 16-bit value
BOOT_UP:       EQU $0000        ; Reset console
DECLSN:        EQU $0190
DECMSN:        EQU $019b
DISPLAY_LOGO:  EQU $1319
MSNTOLSN:      EQU $01a6
```

```
POWER_UP:            EQU $006e
RAND_GEN:            EQU $1ffd ; Output: 16 bit result in RAND_NUM, HL, A=L
RAND_NUM:            EQU $73c8 ; 2 byte output of last call to RAND_GEN
;
; Video related calls
FILL_VRAM:           EQU $1f82
GAME_OPT:            EQU $1f7c
GET_VRAM:            EQU $1fbb
INIT_SPR_NM_TBL:     EQU $1fc1
INIT_TABLE:          EQU $1fb8
LOAD_ASCII:          EQU $1f7f
MODE_1:              EQU $1f85
PUT_VRAM:            EQU $1fbe
READ_REGISTER:       EQU $1fdc
READ_VRAM:           EQU $1fe2
WRITE_REGISTER:      EQU $1fd9
WRITE_VRAM:          EQU $1fdf
WR_SPR_NM_TBL:       EQU $1fc4
;
; Object routines
ACTIVATE:            EQU $1ff7
CALC_OFFSET:         EQU $08c0
GET_BKGRND:          EQU $0898
INIT_WRITER:         EQU $1fe5
PUT_FRAME:           EQU $080b
PUTOBJ:              EQU $1ffa
PUTSEMI:             EQU $06ff
PUT_MOBILE:          EQU $0a87
PUT0SPRITE:          EQU $08df
PUT1SPRITE:          EQU $0955
PUTCOMPLEX:          EQU $0ea2
PX_TO_PTRN_POS:      EQU $07e8
SET_UP_WRITE:        EQU $0623
WRITER:              EQU $1fe8
;
; Graphics primitives
ENLARGE:             EQU $1f73
REFLECT_HORZONTAL:   EQU $1f6d
REFLECT_VERTICAL:    EQU $1f6a
ROTATE_90:           EQU $1f70
;
; Timer related calls
FREE_SIGNAL:         EQU $1fca ; Note: must not be interrupted
INIT_TIMER:          EQU $1fc7 ; **HL=timer table,DE=timer data block
REQUEST_SIGNAL:      EQU $1fcd
TEST_SIGNAL:         EQU $1fd0
TIME_MGR:            EQU $1fd3
AMERICA:             EQU $0069
; Contains how many timer ticks in a second (50/60)
;
; Music/sound effects related
;
PLAY_IT:             EQU $1ff1 ; B=Song number
PLAY_SONGS:          EQU $1f61 ; Call during interrupt (early)
SOUND_INIT:          EQU $1fee ; B=concurrent voices+effects, HL=song table
SOUND_MAN:           EQU $1ff4 ; Call during interrupt (late)
TURN_OFF_SOUND:      EQU $1fd6 ; No sounds
;
; Coleco Controller related calls and settings
;
CONT_READ:           EQU $113d
```

```
CONTROLLER_INIT:    EQU $1105
CONTROLLER_SCAN:    EQU $1f76
DECODER:            EQU $1f79
POLLER:             EQU $1feb
UPDATE_SPINNER:     EQU $1f88
; controller debounce routines
JOY_DBNCE:          EQU $12b9
FIRE_DBNCE:         EQU $1289
ARM_DBNCE:          EQU $12e9
KBD_DBNCE:          EQU $1250
;
; To be added together for CONTROLLER_MAP +0 (player 1),
; and +1 (player 2)
CONTROLLER_ENABLE:  EQU 80h
KEYPAD_ENABLE:      EQU 10h
ARM_BUTTON_ENABLE:  EQU 8
JOYSTICK_ENABLE:    EQU 2
FIRE_BUTTON_ENABLE: EQU 1
;
; Controller Table offsets
PLAYER1:    EQU 0 ; Settings (above)
PLAYER2:    EQU 1
FIRE1:      EQU 2 ; Fire button 1 (40h=yes, 0=no)
JOY1:       EQU 3 ; 1=N, 2=E, 4=S, 8=W, etc.
SPIN1:      EQU 4 ; counter
ARM1:       EQU 5 ; Arm button 1 (40h=yes, 0=no)
KEYPAD1:    EQU 6 ; 0-9, '*'=10, '#'=11
FIRE2:      EQU 7
JOY2:       EQU 8
SPIN2:      EQU 9
ARM2:       EQU 10
KEYPAD2:    EQU 11

StackTop:       EQU $739f ; Top of stack
SPRITE_NAME:    EQU $7030 ; Pointer to sprite name table
; max 32 sprites * 4 bytes each = 128 bytes
; note: 7020h-702bh are used for music player.
SPRITE_ORDER:   EQU $7080 ; Pointer to sprite order table, max 32 sprites
WORK_BUFFER:    EQU $70a0 ; Pointer to graphics work area,
                          ; up to around 300h max usage
;
; Any system values
; VRAM DEFAULT TABLES
VRAM_PATTERN:   EQU $0000
VRAM_NAME:      EQU $1800
VRAM_SPRATTR:   EQU $1B00
VRAM_COLOR:     EQU $2000
VRAM_SPRGEN:    EQU $3800
```

6.2. Library Functions

The next file contains several functions that you might find useful in games you program in the future.

Some of these functions replace the ones that the Coleco BIOS also provides, but I have made some enhancements over the originals.

```
;*******************************************************
; Coleco SUBROUTINES ver 1.02 (C) Electric Adventures 2020
;*******************************************************

; Set address called inside NMI routine
; HL = Hook Address
SET_VDU_HOOK:
    LD A,0cdh
    LD (VDU_HOOK),A
    LD (VDU_HOOK+1),HL
    LD A,0c9h
    LD (VDU_HOOK+3),A
    RET

; Disable the generation of NMI calls
DISABLE_NMI:
    ld      a,(073c4h)
    and     0dfh
DNMI1:
    ld      c,a
    ld      b,1
    jp      01fd9h

; Enable the generation of NMI calls
ENABLE_NMI:
    ld      a,(073c4h)
    or      020h
    call    DNMI1
    jp      01fdch

; Set the name table to default values
; DE = VRAM Offset
SET_DEF_NAME_TBL:
    ld      c,CTRL_PORT
    di
    out     (c),e
    set     6,d
    out     (c),d
    ei
    ld      c,DATA_PORT
    ld      d,3
SDNT1:
    xor     a
SDNT2:
    out     (c),a
    nop
    inc     a
    jp      nz,SDNT2
    dec     d
    jp      nz,SDNT1
    ret
;
```

```
; HL = Source data
; DE = VRAM starting location
RLE2VRAM:
    di
    ld      c,CTRL_PORT
    out     (c),e
    set     6,d
    out     (c),d
    ei
    ld      c,DATA_PORT
RLE2V0:
    ld      a,(hl)
    inc     hl
    cp      0ffh
    ret     z
    bit     7,a
    jr      z,RLE2V2
    and     07fh
    inc     a
    ld      b,a
    ld      a,(hl)
    inc     hl
RLE2V1:
    out     (c),a
    nop
    nop
    djnz    RLE2V1
    jr      RLE2V0
RLE2V2:
    inc     a
    ld      b,a
RLE2V3:
    outi
    jr      z,RLE2V0
    jp      RLE2V3


; Uncompress RLE data into RAM
; HL = Source data
; DE = Destination
RLE2RAM:
RLE2R0:
    ld      a,(hl)
    inc     hl
    cp      0ffh
    ret     z
    bit     7,a
    jr      z,RLE2R2
    and     07fh
    inc     a
    ld      b,a
    ld      a,(hl)
    inc     hl
RLE2R1:
    ld      (de),a
    inc     de
    djnz    RLE2R1
    jr      RLE2R0
RLE2R2:
    inc     a
    ld      b,a
    ldir
```

```
        jr      RLE2R0

; Write to VDP, port in B, value in C
WRTVDP:
    DI
    LD A,B
    OUT (CTRL_PORT),A
    LD A,C
    OR 80h
    OUT (CTRL_PORT),A
    EI
    PUSH HL
    LD A,B
    LD B,0
    LD HL,0F3DFh
    ADD HL,BC
    LD (HL),A
    POP HL
    RET

; Set write to Video RAM
; HL = VRAM Address
SETWRT:
    DI
    LD A,L
    OUT (CTRL_PORT),A
    LD A,H
    AND 3Fh
    OR 40h
    OUT (CTRL_PORT),A
    EI
    RET
;
; Set read to Video RAM
; HL = VRAM Address
SETRD:
    DI
    LD A,L
    OUT (CTRL_PORT),A
    LD A,H
    AND 3Fh
    OUT (CTRL_PORT),A
    EI
    RET

; Load a block of memory to VRAM
; HL = VRAM Address
; DE = RAM Address
; BC = Length
LDIRVM:
    CALL SETWRT
LLOOP:
    LD A,(DE)
    OUT (DATA_PORT),A
    INC DE
    DEC BC
    LD A,C
    OR B
    CP 0
    JR NZ,LLOOP
    RET
```

```
; Fill a section of VRAM with value in A
; HL = VRAM Address
; BC = Length
FILVRM:
    LD E,A
    CALL SETWRT
FLOOP:
    LD A,E
    OUT (DATA_PORT),A
    DEC BC
    LD A,C
    OR B
    CP 0
    JR NZ,FLOOP
    RET


; Write Sprite positions to VRAM
; - writes sprites in reverse order every 2nd screen refresh
; - this allows for eight sprites per line, with flickering
; - only when there are five or more sprites on a line
SPRWRT:
    LD A,(SPRORDER)
    BIT 0,A
    JR NZ,SW1
    ; write sprites normal order
    SET 0,A
    LD (SPRORDER),A
    LD HL,VRAM_SPRATTR
    LD DE,SPRTBL
    LD BC,80h
    CALL LDIRVM
    RET
SW1:
    ; write sprites reverse order
    RES 0,A
    LD (SPRORDER),A
    LD HL,VRAM_SPRATTR
    CALL SETWRT
    LD IX,SPRTBL+80h-4
    LD C,32
SW2:
    LD A,(IX+0)
    OUT (DATA_PORT),A
    LD A,(IX+1)
    OUT (DATA_PORT),A
    LD A,(IX+2)
    OUT (DATA_PORT),A
    LD A,(IX+3)
    OUT (DATA_PORT),A
    DEC IX
    DEC IX
    DEC IX
    DEC IX
    DEC C
    XOR A
    CP C
    JR NZ,SW2
    RET


; Setup Screen 2,2 - Interrupts are disabled
```

```
SETSCREEN2:
    LD BC,0002h         ;Reg 0: Mode 2
    CALL WRITE_REGISTER
    LD BC,0206h         ; Name table 1800h
    CALL WRITE_REGISTER
    LD BC,03ffh         ; Colour table 2000h
    CALL WRITE_REGISTER
    LD BC,0403h         ; Pattern table 0000h
    CALL WRITE_REGISTER
    LD BC,0536h         ; Sprite attribute table 1b00h
    CALL WRITE_REGISTER
    LD BC,0607h         ; Sprite pattern table 3800h
    CALL WRITE_REGISTER
    LD BC,0700h         ; Base colours
    CALL WRITE_REGISTER
    LD BC,01c2h         ; Reg 1: Mode 2, 16k, no interrupts, 16x16 sprites
    CALL WRITE_REGISTER
    RET

; Test for the press of a joystick button (0 or 1)
; A = 255 - fire button pressed
JOYTST:
    CALL POLLER
    LD A,(CONTROLLER_BUFFER+FIRE1)
    OR A
    JR Z,JOYTST2
    LD A,255
    RET
JOYTST2:
    LD A,(CONTROLLER_BUFFER+5)
    AND 040h
    RET Z
    LD A,255
    RET

; Test for a press of a keypad button
JOYPAD:
    CALL POLLER
    LD A,(CONTROLLER_BUFFER+KEYPAD1)
    RET
;
; Test for the direction of joystick 0
; Result: A
JOYDIR:
        CALL POLLER
        LD A,(CONTROLLER_BUFFER+JOY1)
        RET
;
; Play a sound, protects the calling routine from common
; registers being changed.
; B = Sound to play
SOUND:
    PUSH IX
    PUSH IY
    PUSH HL
    PUSH DE
    CALL PLAY_IT
    POP DE
    POP HL
    POP IY
    POP IX
```

```
        RET

; Output a character to the screen name table
; (HL) contains the character to output
PRINTIT:
    XOR A ; clear A
    RLD   ; rotate left out of (HL) into A
    INC A
    OUT (DATA_PORT),A
    DEC A
    RLD   ; rotate left out of (HL) into A
    INC A
    OUT (DATA_PORT),A
    DEC A
    RLD
    RET

; Clear the sprites from the screen (set Y=209)
CLEARSPRITES:
    LD B,80h
    LD DE,SPRTBL
CS1:
    LD A,209
    LD (DE),A
    INC DE
    DEC B
    LD A,B
    CP 0
    JR NZ,CS1
    LD (SPRORDER),A
    RET

; Clear the VDP Pattern table (clears screen)
CLEARPAT:
    LD HL,VRAM_NAME
    LD BC,768
    XOR A
    CALL FILVRM
    RET

; Create and enable standard timers
CREATE_TIMERS:
    LD HL,(AMERICA)        ;How long a second is
    SRA L
    LD H,0
    LD A,1                 ;set to repeating
    CALL REQUEST_SIGNAL
    LD (HalfSecTimer),A    ; Happens once per half second
    LD HL,(AMERICA)        ; How long a second is
    SRA L
    SRA L
    LD H,0
    LD A,1                 ; set to repeating
    CALL REQUEST_SIGNAL
    LD (QtrSecTimer),A     ; Happens once per quarter second
    LD HL,1
    LD A,1                 ; set to repeating
    CALL REQUEST_SIGNAL
    LD (TickTimer),A       ; Happens once per tick
    RET
```

```
;    Seed Random numbers
;    Seed in HL
SEED_RANDOM:
     LD (SEED),HL
     RR H
     RL L
     LD (SEED+2),HL
     RET

;    Generate a random number, based on the initial Seed
;    value.
RND:
     PUSH HL
     PUSH BC
     PUSH DE
     LD DE,(SEED+2)
     LD HL,(SEED)
     LD B,5
RLP1:
     RR H
     RL L
     RR D
     RL E
     DJNZ RLP1
     LD B,3
RLP2:
     PUSH DE
     LD DE,(SEED)
     OR A
     SBC HL,DE
     EX DE,HL
     POP HL
     DJNZ RLP2
     LD (SEED),HL
     LD (SEED+2),DE
     LD A,E
     OR H
     POP DE
     POP BC
     POP HL
     RET

; NMI routine
; - updates a time counter,
; - plays any songs
; - writes in memory sprite table to VDU
; - calls user defined hook - for other writes
; - update the time counters
NMI:
     PUSH  AF
     PUSH  BC
     PUSH  DE
     PUSH  HL
     PUSH  IX
     PUSH  IY
     EX    AF,AF'
     PUSH  AF
     EXX
     PUSH  BC
     PUSH  DE
     PUSH  HL
```

```
    ; update our time counter
    LD HL,(TIME)
    DEC HL
    LD (TIME),HL
    ; Now we can safely call any OS7 calls
    CALL PLAY_SONGS   ; Update active music
    CALL SOUND_MAN    ; Prepare for next go at music
    ; write sprite table
    CALL SPRWRT
    LD A,(VDU_HOOK)
    CP 0cdh
    JR NZ,NMI2
    CALL VDU_HOOK
NMI2:
    CALL TIME_MGR

;Now restore everything
    POP HL
    POP DE
    POP BC
    EXX
    POP AF
    EX AF,AF'
    POP IY
    POP IX
    POP HL
    POP DE
    POP BC

    CALL READ_REGISTER  ;Side effect allows another NMI to happen

    POP AF

    RETN ; Non maskable interrupt used for:
         ; - music, processing timers, sprite motion processing

; Set origin in Coleco RAM area
ORG 07000h ; fit common items before the BIOS RAM usage area

TickTimer:          DS 1 ; Signal that 3 frames has elapsed
HalfSecTimer:       DS 1 ; Signal that 1/2 second has elapsed
QtrSecTimer:        DS 1 ; Signal that 1/4 second has elapsed
TIME:               DS 2
SEED:               DS 4
CONTROLLER_BUFFER:  DS 12 ; Pointer to hand controller input area
MOVDLY:             DS 10 ; Up to 10 movement timers

ORG 07030h ; avoid Coleco BIOS RAM usage area

; Sprite positions
SPRTBL:             DS 80h
SPRORDER:           DS 1  ; flag to indicate the current
                          ; sprite write direction
TIMER_TABLE:        DS 16 ; Pointer to timers table (16 timers)
TIMER_DATA_BLOCK:   DS 58 ; Pointer to timers table for long timers
                          ; 4 bytes * 16 longer than 3 sec timers
VDU_HOOK: DS 4 ; NMI VDU Delayed writes hook
```

6.3. Main Source File

Finally, we have the main source file of our initial template this defines the main logic of, in this case, our demo, or the game you want to program.

It contains the basic start-up and setup of the Coleco such as:

- Setting the screen mode
- Setup the sound chip
- Initialise the controllers
- Defining the patterns and colours of the background tiles
- Defining the patterns used for the sprite objects

```
;************************************************************
; EA Game Template - Coleco ver 1.02 (C) Electric Adventures 2020
;************************************************************
FNAME "TEMPLATE.ROM"
cpu z80
;
; Include Coleco defined values
include "Coleco-Include.ASM"
;
; Set ROM header
            ORG         8000h
;** CARTRIDGE SOFTWARE POINTERS 8000H **
;      ----------------------------------------------
;
      DB 0AAh,055h   ; Cartridge present: ColecoVision logo
      DB 055h,0AAh   ; Cartridge present: skip logo, ColecoVision logo
      DW 0000        ; Pointer to the sprite name table
      DW 0000        ; Pointer to the sprite order table
      DW 0000        ; Pointer to the working buffer for WR_SPR_NM_TBL
      DW CONTROLLER_BUFFER ; Pointer to the hand controller input areas
      DW START       ; Entry point to the user program
;************************************************************

rst_8:
    reti
    nop
rst_10:
    reti
    nop
rst_18:
    JP RAND_GEN
rst_20:
    reti
    nop
rst_28:
    reti
    nop
rst_30:
    reti
    nop
rst_38:
    reti
    nop
    jp NMI

    db "GAME TEMPLATE/ELECTRIC ADVENTURES/2020"
;
```

```
; Start of application logic
START:
    ; set stack pointer
    LD SP,StackTop ;128 bytes in length at 737fh

    ; Initialise sound
    LD B,SoundDataCount   ;Max number of active voices+effects
    LD HL,SoundAddrs
    CALL SOUND_INIT

    ; initialise clock
    LD HL,TIMER_TABLE
    LD DE,TIMER_DATA_BLOCK
    CALL INIT_TIMER

    ; Set screen mode 2,2 (16x16 sprites)
    CALL SETSCREEN2

    CALL CONTROLLER_INIT
    ; Enable both joysticks, buttons, keypads
    LD    HL,09b9bh
    LD    (CONTROLLER_BUFFER),HL

    ; Seed random numbers with a fixed number (nothing else to use?)
    LD HL,1967
    CALL SEED_RANDOM

    ; Enable timers
    CALL CREATE_TIMERS

    ; Do all our VRAM setup
    ; NMI is currently disabled

    ; Send the two sprite definitions to the VDP
    LD HL,VRAM_SPRGEN
    LD DE,SPDATA
    LD BC,32*2
    CALL LDIRVM

    ; Clear the screen
    CALL CLEARPAT

    ; Clear the colour table
    LD HL,VRAM_COLOR
    LD BC,1800h
    LD A,071h ; Cyan on Black
    CALL FILVRM

    ; Load the character set, make all three sections the same
    LD HL,0
SLOOP:
    LD DE,CHRDAT
    PUSH HL
    LD BC,36*8
    CALL LDIRVM
    POP HL
    PUSH HL
    LD BC,VRAM_COLOR
    ADD HL,BC
    ; make numbers yellow
    LD BC,88
```

```
        LD A,0a1h
        CALL FILVRM
        POP HL
        LD BC,800h
        ADD HL,BC
        LD A,H
        CP 18h
        JR C,SLOOP

MAIN_SCREEN:
        ; Read joysticks to clear any false reads
        CALL JOYTST

        ; Initial Seed random numbers with a random number from BIOS
        CALL RAND_GEN
        CALL SEED_RANDOM

        ; disable interrupts
        CALL DISABLE_NMI

        ; Clean up in case the game left anything on screen
        CALL CLEARSPRITES
        CALL SPRWRT

        ; Clear the screen
        CALL CLEARPAT
        LD HL,VRAM_NAME+12
        LD DE,MESG1
        LD BC,8
        CALL LDIRVM

        LD HL,VDU_WRITES
        CALL SET_VDU_HOOK
        CALL ENABLE_NMI

        ; Set initial position, colour and shape of the ball
        LD HL,04040h
        LD (SPRTBL),HL
        LD HL,00500h
        LD (SPRTBL+2),HL

        ; Set initial position, colour and shape of the bat
        LD HL,080A0H
        LD (SPRTBL+4),HL
        LD HL,00604h
        LD (SPRTBL+6),HL

        ; set initial velocity of ball (dx = 1, dy = 1)
        LD HL,00101h
        LD (BALL),HL

        ; Main game logic loop
MLOOP:
        ; check that a base tick has occurred
        ; ensures consistent movement speed between 50 & 60Hz systems
        LD A,(TickTimer)
        CALL TEST_SIGNAL
        OR A
        JR Z,MLOOP

        CALL MOVE_BALL
```

```
        CALL MOVE_PLAYER
        JR MLOOP

; Move the player
MOVE_PLAYER:
        CALL JOYDIR
        BIT 1,A
        JR Z,NRIGHT
        ; move to the right
        LD A,(SPRTBL+5)
        CP 239
        RET Z
        INC A
        LD (SPRTBL+5),A
        RET
NRIGHT:
        BIT 3,A
        RET Z
        ; move to the left
        LD A,(SPRTBL+5)
        CP 0
        RET Z
        DEC A
        LD (SPRTBL+5),A
        RET

; move the Ball
MOVE_BALL:
        ; change the current y position
        LD A,(SPRTBL)
        LD B,A
        LD A,(BALL)
        ADD A,B
        LD (SPRTBL),A
        CP 0
        JR NZ, NOTTOP
        ; hit the top
        LD A,1
        LD (BALL),A
        LD B,1
        CALL PLAY_IT
        JR YDONE
NOTTOP:
        CP 175
        JR NZ, YDONE
        LD A,255
        LD (BALL),A
        LD B,1
        CALL PLAY_IT
YDONE:
        ; change the current x position
        LD A,(SPRTBL+1)
        LD B,A
        LD A,(BALL+1)
        ADD A,B
        LD (SPRTBL+1),A
        CP 0
        JR NZ, NOTLEFT
        ; hit the left
        LD A,1
        LD (BALL+1),A
```

```
        LD B,1
        CALL PLAY_IT
        JR XDONE
NOTLEFT:
        CP 239
        JR NZ, XDONE
        LD A,255
        LD (BALL+1),A
        LD B,1
        CALL PLAY_IT
XDONE:
        RET

; This is our routine called every VDP interrupt
; - Do all VDP writes here to avoid corruption
; Note:
; - The included VDP routine is already calling the sound update
;   routines, and writing the sprite data table to VRAM.
VDU_WRITES:
        RET

CHRDAT:
        DB 000,000,000,000,000,000,000,000 ; 0  blank
        DB 124,198,198,198,198,198,124,000 ; 1  '0'
        DB 024,056,120,024,024,024,024,000 ; 2  '1'
        DB 124,198,006,004,024,096,254,000 ; 3  '2'
        DB 124,198,006,060,006,198,124,000 ; 4  '3'
        DB 024,056,088,152,254,024,024,000 ; 5  '4'
        DB 254,192,192,252,006,198,124,000 ; 6  '5'
        DB 124,198,192,252,198,198,124,000 ; 7  '6'
        DB 254,006,012,012,024,024,024,000 ; 8  '7'
        DB 124,198,198,124,198,198,124,000 ; 9  '8'
        DB 124,198,198,126,006,198,124,000 ; 10 '9'
        DB 056,108,198,198,254,198,198,000 ; 11 'A'
        DB 252,198,198,252,198,198,252,000 ; 12 'B'
        DB 124,230,192,192,192,230,124,000 ; 13 'C'
        DB 252,206,198,198,198,206,252,000 ; 14 'D'
        DB 254,192,192,248,192,192,254,000 ; 15 'E'
        DB 254,192,192,248,192,192,192,000 ; 16 'F'
        DB 124,198,192,192,206,198,124,000 ; 17 'G'
        DB 198,198,198,254,198,198,198,000 ; 18 'H'
        DB 254,056,056,056,056,056,254,000 ; 19 'I'
        DB 126,024,024,024,216,216,248,000 ; 20 'J'
        DB 198,204,216,240,248,204,198,000 ; 21 'K'
        DB 192,192,192,192,192,192,254,000 ; 22 'L'
        DB 130,198,238,254,214,198,198,000 ; 23 'M'
        DB 134,198,230,214,206,198,194,000 ; 24 'N'
        DB 124,238,198,198,198,238,124,000 ; 25 'O'
        DB 252,198,198,252,192,192,192,000 ; 26 'P'
        DB 124,198,198,198,214,206,124,000 ; 27 'Q'
        DB 252,198,198,252,248,204,198,000 ; 28 'R'
        DB 124,198,192,124,006,198,124,000 ; 29 'S'
        DB 254,056,056,056,056,056,056,000 ; 30 'T'
        DB 198,198,198,198,198,238,124,000 ; 31 'U'
        DB 198,198,198,238,108,108,056,000 ; 32 'V'
        DB 198,198,214,254,124,108,040,000 ; 33 'X'
        DB 198,238,124,056,124,238,198,000 ; 34 'Y'
        DB 198,238,124,056,056,056,056,000 ; 35 'Z'

MESG1: ; Template
        DB 030,015,023,026,022,011,030,015
```

```
SPDATA:
    db 003h,00Fh,01Fh,03Fh,07Fh,07Fh,0FFh,0FFh
    db 0FFh,0FFh,07Fh,07Fh,03Fh,01Fh,00Fh,003h
    db 0C0h,0F0h,0F8h,0FCh,0FEh,0FEh,0FFh,0FFh
    db 0FFh,0FFh,0FEh,0FEh,0FCh,0F8h,0F0h,0C0h
    db 000,000,000,000,000,000,000,000
    db 000,000,000,000,000,000,255,255
    db 000,000,000,000,000,000,000,000
    db 000,000,000,000,000,000,255,255

;***************************
; Sound and music data area
;***************************

; Bounce
bounce:
    DB 081h, 054h, 010h, 002h, 023h, 007h
    DB $90  ; end
    DW 0000h

;***************************
; Sound settings
;***************************
SoundDataCount:     EQU 7
Len_SoundDataArea:  EQU 10*SoundDataCount+1 ; 7 data areas
SoundAddrs:
    DW bounce,SoundDataArea     ; 1  ball bounce sound
    DW 0,0

;***************************
; Standard Libraries
;***************************

include "Coleco-Lib.ASM"

;***************************
; RAM Definitions
;***************************

BALL:       DS 2

; Sound Data area - 7 songs
SoundDataArea: DS Len_SoundDataArea
```

7. Starting a Game

In this chapter we are going to start making our game, called "Mega Blast", this game is based on the Intellivision game called Astro Smash, a simple space shooting game with our 'hero' ship down at the bottom of the screen, and various 'enemies' dropping down towards the bottom of the screen.

Figure 11 – Astro Smash on the Intellivision

To get things started we are going to go through:

- Initialising our graphics
- Displaying the graphics on both our title screen and then the main screen of the game

I have included the complete code for this section in the GitHub repository, so you can follow through the various steps without having to worry about typing in code.

The supplied code has two folders, "Start" (based on the template code in the previous chapter), where we start in this chapter and "End" (the final code) and a copy of the ROM file.

7.1. Preparing the template

Starting with the template project introduced in the last chapter, we need to make some changes, before we get started.

Once again this is included here for completeness, if you have access to the downloadable content, these changes will be available in the Start folder for this chapter.

Copy the template files into a fresh directory and rename the "template.asm" file to Coleco-MegaBlast.asm.

Open the file and replace the first few lines with the following:

```
;*****************************************************************
;
; MegaBlast - Coleco ver 1.00 (C) Electric Adventures 2020
;
;*****************************************************************
FNAME "MEGABLAST.ROM"
```

Other than changing the text in the comment section, this changes the name of the ROM file that will be created to MEGABLAST.ROM.

Note: Exclude this line if using the Glass assembler

Going down a couple of lines add some values we will use later as follows:

```
; Include Coleco defined values
include "Coleco-Include.ASM"

PATSIZE:     EQU 71
SPRITECOUNT: EQU 11
```

And just before the **START:** label change the game rom title as follows:

```
        db "MEGA BLAST/ELECTRIC ADVENTURES/2020"
;
; Start of application logic
START:
```

Find the following line:

```
; Enable timers.
CALL CREATE_TIMERS
```

Remove all the lines after that code, up to the **MAIN_SCREEN** label.

So, our random numbers are a bit more random, just after the **MAIN_SCREEN** label replace the call to RAND_GEN with the following:

```
MAIN_SCREEN:
    ; Read joysticks to clear any false reads
    CALL JOYTST

    ; Initial Seed random with the time that has passed
    LD HL,(TIME)
    CALL SEED_RANDOM
```

Remove the following code, just before the MLOOP label:

```
        ; Clear the screen
        CALL CLEARPAT
        LD HL,VRAM_NAME+12
        LD DE,MESG1
        LD BC,8
        CALL LDIRVM


        LD HL,VDU_WRITES
        CALL SET_VDU_HOOK
        CALL ENABLE_NMI

        ; Set initial position, colour and shape of the ball
        LD HL,04040h
        LD (SPRTBL),HL
        LD HL,00500h
        LD (SPRTBL+2),HL

        ; Set initial position, colour and shape of the bat
        LD HL,080A0H
        LD (SPRTBL+4),HL
        LD HL,00604h
        LD (SPRTBL+6),HL

        ; set initial velocity of ball (dx = 1, dy = 1)
        LD HL,00101h
        LD (BALL),HL

        ; Main game logic loop
MLOOP:
```

Remove the following lines after the MLOOP: label as follows:

```
MLOOP:
        ; check that a base tick has occurred
        ; ensures consistent movement speed between 50 & 60Hz systems
        LD A,(TickTimer)
        CALL TEST_SIGNAL
        OR A
        JR Z,MLOOP

        CALL MOVE_BALL
        CALL MOVE_PLAYER
        JR MLOOP
```

Remove the functions **MOVE_PLAYER** and **MOVE_BALL** and the data sections labelled **CHRDAT**, **MESG1** and **SPDATA**.

One final thing, at the end of the file, after the ORG RAMSTART remove the ram definition for BALL: as follows:

```
ORG RAMSTART

BALL:       DS 2
```

You should now be able to assemble the code and are ready to move on to the next section.

7.2.Initialising our graphics

Using the latest version of my MSX Sprite & Tile Editor application, I have designed both the sprites and tiles we will need to get our application started.

From this tool, after opening the supplied file, you can save the file in assembler format.

The resultant file (Coleco-MegaBlast-Tileset.ASM) can be used directly in our project as an included file. That way, if you want to change any of the graphics, you can do so in the editor, resave the file, run the assembler and they will be updated in your game.

The information that defines our sprites and tiles is now in our game, but they need to be transferred from our ROM into the video processor's RAM (or VRAM as it's called).

To make this easier to read I have added a function (section of code) as follows:

```
; Load the character set, make all three sections the same
LOAD_CHR_SET:
    LD HL,0
SLOOP:
    LD DE,TILESET_1_PAT
    PUSH HL
    LD BC,PATSIZE*8
    CALL LDIRVM
    POP HL
    ; now load colour attributes
    PUSH HL
    LD BC,VRAM_COLOR
    ADD HL,BC
    LD DE,TILESET_1_COL
    LD BC,PATSIZE*8
    CALL LDIRVM
    POP HL
    LD BC,800h
    ADD HL,BC
    LD A,H
    CP 18h
    JR C,SLOOP
    RET
```

Note: I am keeping this simple, i.e., no compression, and we only use one set of tiles for each of the three regions on the screen.

This function basically grabs the tile data saved in the design tool and copies it to the VRAM so the video processor will use it to draw our background.

7.3. Displaying Our Title Screen

We then need to call this code to load our pattern (and colour) data into VRAM as follows:

So just after:

```
; Enable timers.
CALL CREATE_TIMERS
```

We add the following code:

```
TITLESCREEN:
    ; display our title screen
    CALL DISABLE_NMI
    ; Clear the screen
    CALL CLEARPAT

    ; Load the character set, make all three sections the same
    CALL LOAD_CHR_SET

    ; now setup the title screen layout
    LD HL,VRAM_NAME
    LD DE,TITLE_SCREEN_PAT
    LD BC,24*32
    CALL LDIRVM

    CALL JOYTST ; clear joystick buffer
    LD HL,OUTPUT_VDP_TITLE
    CALL SET_VDU_HOOK
    CALL ENABLE_NMI

SPLASH_TITLE2:
    CALL JOYTST
    CP 255
    JR Z,NGAME
    LD A,(HalfSecTimer)
    CALL TEST_SIGNAL
    OR A
    JR Z,SPLASH_TITLE2
    ; Any other actions on the title screen go here
    JR SPLASH_TITLE2

NGAME:
    CALL DISABLE_NMI
    CALL INITRAM
```

We also add a section of data near the bottom of our code i.e. after:

```
; This is our routine called every VDP interrupt during normal game play
; - Do all VDP writes here to avoid corruption
VDU_WRITES:
    RET
```

We add this section of tile layout data:

```
; This is our routine called every VDP interrupt during the title screen
; - Do all VDP writes here to avoid corruption
OUTPUT_VDP_TITLE:
    RET


; Init Ram for a new game
INITRAM:
    RET


TITLE_SCREEN_PAT:
    DB 000,000,000,000,000,000,000,000,000,000,000,000,000,000,000,000
    DB 000,000,000,000,000,000,000,000,000,000,000,000,000,000,000,000
    DB 000,000,000,000,000,000,000,000,000,000,000,000,000,000,000,000
    DB 000,000,000,000,000,000,000,000,000,000,000,000,000,000,000,000
    DB 000,000,000,000,000,000,000,000,000,000,000,000,000,000,000,000
    DB 000,000,000,000,000,000,000,000,000,000,000,000,000,000,000,000
    DB 000,000,000,000,000,000,000,000,000,000,000,000,000,000,000,000
    DB 000,000,000,000,000,000,000,000,000,000,000,000,000,000,000,000
    DB 000,000,000,000,000,023,000,015,000,017,000,011,000,000,000,000
    DB 012,000,022,000,011,000,029,000,030,000,000,000,000,000,000,000
    DB 000,000,000,000,000,000,000,000,000,000,000,000,000,000,000,000
    DB 000,000,000,000,000,000,000,000,000,000,000,000,000,000,000,000
    DB 000,000,000,000,000,000,000,000,000,000,000,000,000,000,000,000
    DB 000,000,000,000,000,000,000,000,000,000,000,000,000,000,000,000
    DB 000,000,000,000,000,000,000,000,000,000,000,000,000,000,000,000
    DB 000,000,000,000,000,000,000,000,000,000,000,000,000,000,000,000
    DB 000,000,000,000,000,000,000,000,000,000,000,000,000,000,000,000
    DB 000,000,000,000,000,000,000,000,000,000,000,000,000,000,000,000
    DB 000,000,000,000,000,000,000,000,000,000,000,000,000,000,000,000
    DB 000,000,000,000,000,000,000,000,000,000,000,000,000,000,000,000
    DB 000,000,000,000,000,000,000,000,000,000,000,000,000,000,000,000
    DB 000,000,000,000,000,000,000,000,000,000,000,000,000,000,000,000
    DB 000,000,000,000,000,000,000,000,000,000,000,000,000,000,000,000
    DB 000,000,000,000,000,000,000,000,000,000,000,000,000,000,000,000
    DB 000,000,000,000,000,000,000,000,000,000,000,000,000,000,000,000
    DB 000,000,000,000,000,000,000,000,000,000,000,000,000,000,000,000
    DB 000,000,000,000,000,000,000,000,000,000,000,000,000,000,000,000
    DB 000,000,000,000,000,000,000,000,000,000,000,000,000,000,000,000
    DB 000,000,000,000,000,000,000,000,000,000,000,000,000,000,000,000
    DB 000,000,000,000,000,000,000,000,000,000,000,000,000,000,000,000
    DB 000,000,000,000,000,000,000,000,000,000,000,000,000,000,000,000
    DB 000,000,000,000,000,000,000,000,000,000,000,000,000,000,000,000
    DB 037,038,039,040,037,038,039,040,037,038,039,040,037,038,039,040
    DB 037,038,039,040,037,038,039,040,037,038,039,040,037,038,039,040
    DB 000,000,000,000,000,000,000,000,000,000,000,000,000,000,000,000
    DB 000,000,000,000,000,000,000,000,000,000,000,000,000,000,000,000
    DB 000,000,000,000,000,000,000,000,000,000,000,000,000,000,000,000
    DB 000,000,000,000,000,000,000,000,000,000,000,000,000,000,000,000
; press fire to begin
    DB 000,000,000,000,000,000,026,028,015,029,029,000,016,019,028,015
    DB 000,030,025,000,012,015,017,019,024,000,000,000,000,000,000,000
    DB 000,000,000,000,000,000,000,000,000,000,000,000,000,000,000,000
    DB 000,000,000,000,000,000,000,000,000,000,000,000,000,000,000,000
    DB 000,000,000,000,000,000,000,000,000,000,000,000,000,000,000,000
    DB 000,000,000,000,000,000,000,000,000,000,000,000,000,000,000,000
; EA Logo
    DB 061,061,061,061,061,061,061,061,061,061,061,057,058,059,060,061
```

```
DB  062,063,064,065,066,061,061,061,061,061,061,061,061,061,061,061
```

And include our sprite and tile data straight after:

```
;*********************************************************************
;  Include external data files
;*********************************************************************

include "Coleco-MegaBlast-Tileset.ASM"
```

You should now be able to build and run the resultant "MegaBlast.rom" file using BlueMSX and see the title screen as follows:

Figure 12 - Our initial title screen as displayed on BlueMSX

7.4. Displaying Our Game Screen

Next, we can display the main screen of our game.

First let's add the tile layout data for the screen below the one we added previously as follows:

```
MAINLAYOUT:
    DB 000,000,000,000,000,000,000,000,000,000,000,000,000,000,000,000
    DB 000,000,000,000,000,000,000,000,000,000,000,000,000,000,000,000
    DB 000,000,000,000,000,000,000,000,000,000,000,000,000,000,000,000
    DB 000,000,000,000,000,000,000,000,000,000,000,000,000,000,000,000
    DB 000,000,000,000,000,000,000,000,000,000,000,000,000,000,000,000
    DB 000,000,000,000,000,000,000,000,000,000,000,000,000,000,000,000
    DB 000,000,000,000,000,000,000,000,000,000,000,000,000,000,000,000
    DB 000,000,000,000,000,000,000,000,000,000,000,000,000,000,000,000
    DB 000,000,000,000,000,000,000,000,000,000,000,000,000,000,000,000
    DB 000,000,000,000,000,000,000,000,000,000,000,000,000,000,000,000
    DB 000,000,000,000,000,000,000,000,000,000,000,000,000,000,000,000
    DB 000,000,000,000,000,000,000,000,000,000,000,000,000,000,000,000
    DB 000,000,000,000,000,000,000,000,000,000,000,000,000,000,000,000
    DB 000,000,000,000,000,000,000,000,000,000,000,000,000,000,000,000
    DB 000,000,000,000,000,000,000,000,000,000,000,000,000,000,000,000
    DB 000,000,000,000,000,000,000,000,000,000,000,000,000,000,000,000
    DB 000,000,000,000,000,000,000,000,000,000,000,000,000,000,000,000
    DB 000,000,000,000,000,000,000,000,000,000,000,000,000,000,000,000
    DB 000,000,000,000,000,000,000,000,000,000,000,000,000,000,000,000
    DB 000,000,000,000,000,000,000,000,000,000,000,000,000,000,000,000
    DB 000,000,000,000,000,000,000,000,000,000,000,000,000,000,000,000
    DB 000,000,000,000,000,000,000,000,000,000,000,000,000,000,000,000
    DB 000,000,000,000,000,000,000,000,000,000,000,000,000,000,000,000
    DB 000,000,000,000,000,000,000,000,000,000,000,000,000,000,000,000
    DB 000,000,000,000,000,000,000,000,000,000,000,000,000,000,000,000
    DB 000,000,000,000,000,000,000,000,000,000,000,000,000,000,000,000
    DB 000,000,000,000,000,000,000,000,000,000,000,000,000,000,000,000
    DB 000,000,000,000,000,000,000,000,000,000,000,000,000,000,000,000
    DB 000,000,000,000,000,000,000,000,000,000,000,000,000,000,000,000
    DB 000,000,000,000,000,000,000,000,000,000,000,000,000,000,000,000
    DB 000,000,000,000,000,000,000,000,000,000,000,000,000,000,000,000
    DB 000,000,000,000,000,000,000,000,000,000,000,000,000,000,000,000
    DB 037,038,039,040,037,038,039,040,037,038,039,040,037,038,039,040
    DB 037,038,039,040,037,038,039,040,037,038,039,040,037,038,039,040
    DB 000,000,000,000,000,000,000,000,000,000,000,000,000,000,000,000
    DB 000,000,000,000,000,000,000,000,000,000,000,000,000,000,000,000
    DB 000,000,000,000,000,000,000,000,000,000,000,000,000,000,000,000
    DB 000,000,000,000,000,000,000,000,000,000,000,000,000,000,000,000
; planet surface
    DB 041,041,041,041,041,041,041,041,041,041,041,041,041,041,041,041
    DB 041,041,041,041,041,041,041,041,041,041,041,041,041,041,041,041
; score and life area
    DB 000,000,000,000,000,000,000,000,000,000,000,000,000,000,000,000
    DB 000,000,000,000,000,000,000,000,000,000,000,000,000,000,000,000
    DB 000,000,000,001,001,001,001,001,001,001,000,000,000,000,000,000
    DB 000,000,000,000,000,000,000,000,000,000,000,000,000,000,000,000
; EA Logo
    DB 061,061,061,061,061,061,061,061,061,061,061,057,058,059,060,061
    DB 062,063,064,065,066,061,061,061,061,061,061,061,061,061,061,061
```

And now just after:

```
NGAME:
      CALL DISABLE_NMI
      CALL INITRAM
```

We can add code to copy both our sprite and tile patterns to VRAM and then set up the layout for the main screen of the game as follows:

```
      ; Send the sprite definitions to the VDP
      LD HL,VRAM_SPRGEN
      LD DE,MAIN_SHIP
      LD BC,32*SPRITECOUNT
      CALL LDIRVM

      ; Load the character set, make all three sections the same
      CALL LOAD_CHR_SET
```

After the MAIN_SCREEN: label and replace the section of code:

```
      ; Clear the screen
      CALL CLEARPAT

      ; Main game logic loop
MLOOP:
      ; check that a base tick has occurred
      ; ensures consistent movement speed between 50 & 60Hz systems
      LD A,(TickTimer)
      CALL TEST_SIGNAL
      OR A
      JR Z,MLOOP

      JR MLOOP
```

With this section:

```
      ; now setup the main screen layout
      LD HL,VRAM_NAME
      LD DE,MAINLAYOUT
      LD BC,24*32
      CALL LDIRVM

      ; set position of player ship
      LD A,150
      LD (SPRTBL),A
      LD (SPRTBL+4),A
      LD A,120
      LD (SPRTBL+1),A
      LD (SPRTBL+5),A
      XOR A
      LD (SPRTBL+2),A
      LD A,4
      LD (SPRTBL+6),A
      LD A,05h
      LD (SPRTBL+3),A
      LD A,0fh
      LD (SPRTBL+7),A

      LD HL,VDU_WRITES
```

```
        CALL SET_VDU_HOOK
        CALL ENABLE_NMI

        ; Main game logic loop
MLOOP:
        ; check that a base tick has occurred
        ; ensures consistent movement speed between 50 & 60Hz systems
        LD A,(TickTimer)
        CALL TEST_SIGNAL
        OR A
        JR Z,MLOOP2
        ; once per tick

MLOOP2:
        LD A,(QtrSecTimer)
        CALL TEST_SIGNAL
        OR A
        JR Z,MLOOP

        JR MLOOP
```

After you build and run the ROM in BlueMSX you should end up with a game screen (after you press fire on the title screen) as follows:

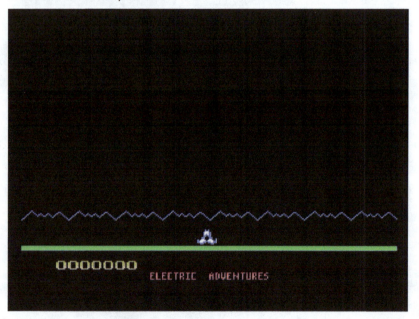

Figure 13 - Our main game screen

8. Move and Shoot

In this chapter, we are going to get some objects moving on the screen by:

- Testing the joystick direction and moving the player ship left or right
- Testing the joystick fire button and placing a bullet on screen
- Moving the current player bullet up the screen.

I have included the complete code for this section, so you can follow through the various steps without having to worry about typing in code.

The supplied code has two folders, Start, where we start in this chapter and End, the final code, and a copy of the ROM file.

8.1. Moving the Player's Ship

Our first step is to add some code to look at the position of the joystick controller and move the player's ship left or right in response.

Player moves from side to side

Figure 14 - Player ship movement

Find the following section of code, that handles our main game logic loop and add a call to a new function called '**MOVE_PLAYER**' as highlighted below:

```
; Main game logic loop
MLOOP:
    ; check that a base tick has occurred
    ; ensures consistent movement speed between 50 & 60Hz systems
    LD A, (TickTimer)
    CALL TEST_SIGNAL
    OR A
    JR Z, MLOOP2
    ; once per tick
    CALL MOVE_PLAYER

MLOOP2:
    LD A, (QtrSecTimer)
    CALL TEST_SIGNAL
    OR A
```

```
        JR Z,MLOOP

        JR MLOOP
```

This code will be called every time the screen has been drawn, i.e. a vertical blank has occurred.

We will not be drawing anything, just changing the stored location of items, so we don't need to be inside the interrupt routine.

Note: Trying to draw anything to the screen outside of the interrupt routine can cause on screen corruption.

Next, we need to add our new function that does the work of looking at the joystick and moving the ship sprite right or left by one pixel depending on the direction of the joystick. It also checks the current position of the ship so that our movement stops at either the left or right of the screen.

```
    ; Detect joystick direction and move the player accordingly
MOVE_PLAYER:
        CALL JOYDIR
        LD C,A
        BIT 1,C
        JR Z,NRIGHT
        ; move to the right
        LD A,(SPRTBL+1)
        CP 242
        JR NC,NLEFT
        INC A
        LD (SPRTBL+1),A
        LD (SPRTBL+5),A
        JR NLEFT
NRIGHT:
        BIT 3,C
        JR Z,NLEFT
        ; move to the left
        LD A,(SPRTBL+1)
        CP 0
        JR Z,NLEFT
        DEC A
        LD (SPRTBL+1),A
        LD (SPRTBL+5),A
NLEFT:
        RET
```

8.2. Firing a player bullet

Next, we need to look at the joystick trigger and if we haven't already fired a bullet, place a bullet sprite on the screen.

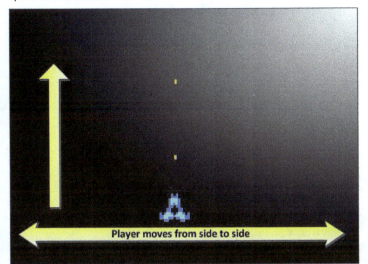

Figure 15 - Player shot firing and movement

First, we add our function call just after our previous one as follows:

```
LD A,(TickTimer)
CALL TEST_SIGNAL
OR A
JR Z,MLOOP2
; once per tick
CALL MOVE_PLAYER
CALL FIRE_PLAYER_BULLET
```

And add the function code as follows:

```
        ; Check for player bullet firing
FIRE_PLAYER_BULLET:
        ; make sure there is not already a bullet
        LD A,(SPRTBL+8)
        CP 209
        RET NZ
        ; see if the fire button is pressed
        CALL JOYTST
        CP 0
        RET Z
        ; fire bullet
        ; set Y based on player ship
        LD A,(SPRTBL)
        SUB 6
        LD (SPRTBL+8),A
        ; set X based on player ship
        LD A,(SPRTBL+1)
        ADD A,6
        LD (SPRTBL+9),A
        ; set bullet sprite pattern
```

```
LD A,24
LD (SPRTBL+10),A
; set bullet colour
LD A,11
LD (SPRTBL+11),A
RET
```

This first checks to make sure we don't already have a bullet sprite on the screen.

Then if the joystick button is pressed, a bullet sprite is placed on the screen relative to the current position of the player's ship.

8.3. Move the Player Bullet

Next, we need to add code to move the player bullet up the screen until it hits the top.

So, we first add a call to a new function called '**MOVE_PLAYER_BULLET**' just below our previous two calls as follows:

```
LD A,(TickTimer)
CALL TEST_SIGNAL
OR A
JR Z,MLOOP2
; once per tick
CALL MOVE_PLAYER
CALL FIRE_PLAYER_BULLET
CALL MOVE_PLAYER_BULLET
```

Add our function code as follows:

```
; Move the players bullet
MOVE_PLAYER_BULLET:
    ; check that the bullet is visible
    LD A,(SPRTBL+8)
    CP 209
    RET Z
    ; decrease bullets Y position
    DEC A
    DEC A
    DEC A
    CP 4
    JR NC, MPB1
    ; bullet has reached the top of the screen, hide the bullet
    LD A,209
MPB1:
    ; save new position
    LD (SPRTBL+8),A
    RET
```

This function first checks whether the player bullet sprite is on the screen, then if so, decreases its Y position by 3 pixels.

If it has reached the top of the screen, it is removed. Otherwise, the sprite location is updated in RAM (ready to be copied to VRAM at the next NMI).

9. Enemy Movement

In the Intellivision game of Astro Smash, that we are basing our game on, the main enemies are Asteroids that fall down the screen, exploding when they hit the ground.

Points are awarded to the player, when one is destroyed, and points are removed if one reaches the planet surface.

In this chapter we are going to introduce some simple enemy movement.

This will involve:

- Using a random number generator to determine when an asteroid should appear and at what speed.
- Moving any visible asteroids towards the bottom of the screen.
- Detecting when an asteroid reaches the bottom of the screen.

9.1. Step One – Asteroid Generation

Our first step is to determine when new asteroids should appear at the top of the screen, to do this we use a random number generator, along with our current difficulty level to work out whether one appears and another random value to work out how far across the screen it will appear.

The supplied template code includes a random number function that uses a time counter, which starts when the computer/console first starts.

Randomness is introduced in the amount of time between starting up and when the user presses a button on the controller to start the game.

This initial time value is called the Seed of our random number sequence of numbers. Yes, that's right, computer-based random numbers are a sequence of numbers that are generated from a set of calculations.

As computer chips have become more complex, random number generation has been able to produce larger sets of random numbers, but for our 8-bit game we don't need anything too complex, just random enough to introduce some uncertainty in enemy behaviour to the player.

Random Number Functions

There are two functions defined in the supplied template library as follows:

SEED_RANDOM – The random number Seed value in the register HL is stored in memory as a 32-bit number.

RND – This returns the next number (from 0 to 255) in the random number sequenced based on the current Seed value.

The ColecoVision BIOS also has a decent random number generator. See RAND_GEN for more details.

Setup Code

In our current code there are already two parts of our random number setup code, just after the START: tag as follows:

```
START:

    ...

    ; Seed random numbers with a fixed number
    LD HL,1967
    CALL SEED_RANDOM
```

This sets the seed at a known value, rather than just being zero, for any random numbers needed during our title screen and setup phase.

Then just after the **MAIN_SCREEN** tag, we set the Seed to the amount of time that has passed since the game code started and when the player presses the fire button as follows:

```
MAIN_SCREEN:
    ; Read joysticks to clear any false reads
    CALL JOYTST

    LD HL,(TIME)
    CALL SEED_RANDOM
```

Now before we go too far, we need some new areas of RAM set aside. So, at the end of our source file we need to add two variables as follows:

```
ORG RAMSTART

LEVEL:          DS 1
ENEMYDATA:      DS 20
ANIMATE:        DS 1
```

These new areas of RAM need to be initialised to zero, so we have a known starting point as follows:

```
; Init RAM for a new game
INITRAM:
    XOR A
    LD (LEVEL),A
    LD (ANIMATE),A
    ; initialise enemy data
    LD HL,ENEMYDATA
    LD (HL),A
    LD DE,ENEMYDATA+1
    LD BC,19
    LDIR
    RET
```

The LEVEL variable needs to be initialised in our NGAME section of code as follows:

```
NGAME:
    CALL DISABLE_NMI
    CALL INITRAM
    ; Set initial LEVEL
    LD A,1
    LD (LEVEL),A
```

Generate Enemies

Now we have our random number generator set up, let's add a new function to our main game loop that will spawn new enemies. For the moment, it will just be asteroids, but later we can add more enemy types.

Add the call to our new function **SPAWN_ENEMIES** after our other action calls in our main loop as follows:

```
    ; Main game logic loop
MLOOP:
    ; check that a base tick has occurred
    ; ensures consistent movement speed between 50 & 60Hz systems
    LD A,(TickTimer)
    CALL TEST_SIGNAL
    OR A
    JR Z,MLOOP2
    ; once per tick
    CALL MOVE_PLAYER
    CALL FIRE_PLAYER_BULLET
    CALL MOVE_PLAYER_BULLET
    CALL SPAWN_ENEMIES
MLOOP2:
    LD A,(QtrSecTimer)
    CALL TEST_SIGNAL
    OR A
    JR Z,MLOOP

    JR MLOOP
```

Now just after our other main loop functions add our **SPAWN_ENEMIES** function as follows:

```
    ; Spawn/create new enemies
SPAWN_ENEMIES:
    LD A,(LEVEL)
    INC A
    SLA A ; multiply by 4
    SLA A
    LD C,A
    CALL RND
    CP C
    RET NC
    ; see if there is an enemy object available
    LD HL,ENEMYDATA
    LD B,20
SE1:
    XOR A
    CP (HL)
    JR NZ,SE2
    ; enemy available
```

```
        PUSH HL
        ; calc our sprite memory position
        LD A,20
        SUB B
        SLA A
        SLA A
        LD C,A
        LD B,0
        LD HL,SPRTBL+12
        ADD HL,BC
        ; set Y to zero
        LD A,0
        LD (HL),A
        ; set X to a random value
        INC HL
        CALL RND
        LD (HL),A
        ; set pattern
        INC HL
        LD A,8
        LD (HL),A
        ; set colour
        INC HL
        LD A,0dh
        LD (HL),A
        POP DE
        LD A,1
        LD (DE),A
        RET
SE2:
        ; move to the next data position
        INC HL
        ; dec b and jump if non-zero
        DJNZ SE1
        RET
```

This is a bit more complex function than we have gone through previously, so I will step through what it does as follows:

1. Use the current level to work out a low number (that increases with our level of difficulty)
2. Call our random number generator, which will give us a number between 0 and 255, if that number is less than the number, we worked out in step 1, we want to try and create a new enemy.
3. We can't have unlimited enemies on the screen, so I have set a limit of 20 (which should be plenty), and for each one we have a byte of memory set aside to control whether it is on the screen (and, later on, what type of enemy).

   In this step, we search our list of enemies until we find one that is not currently on screen.
4. We have used two sprites for our main ship, and one sprite for our player bullet, so the next 20 sprites we can use for the enemy objects.

   In this step, we work out the starting address of our local memory holding the definition of the sprite we want to use.
5. We set the Y position to 0, i.e. the top of the screen
6. We set the X position using our random number function, i.e. 0-255 (we can adjust this a bit later if it doesn't quite suit).
7. We set our sprite starting pattern (16x16 sprites use four 8x8 patterns)
8. We set our sprite colour (0Dh – which is purple – no browns in most of the Z80 systems)
9. Lastly, we store a 1 in our enemy byte, so we know it is in use.

9.2.Step Two – Enemy Movement

Our next step is to make the enemy objects that are currently on screen move, to start with we will just make them move straight down the screen.

After our call to **SPAWN_ENEMIES** add a new call to **MOVE_ENEMIES** as follows:

```
CALL SPAWN_ENEMIES
CALL MOVE_ENEMIES
```

Next add the new **MOVE_ENEMIES** function as follows:

```
; Move any active enemies
MOVE_ENEMIES:
    LD HL,ENEMYDATA
    LD B,20
ME1:
    XOR A
    CP (HL)
    JR Z,ME2
    ; found active enemy
    PUSH BC
    ; calc our sprite memory position
    LD A,20
    SUB B
    SLA A
    SLA A
    LD C,A
    LD B,0
    LD IX,SPRTBL+12
    ADD IX,BC
    POP BC
    ; animate our enemy pattern
    LD A,(ANIMATE)
    CP 0
    JR NZ,ME5 ; do we need to animate?
    ; animate our sprite pattern (hardwired for the moment)
    LD A,(IX+2) ; get current pattern
    ADD A,4      ; add four
    CP 16
    JR NZ,ME4   ; if we have reached 16 we need to move
                ; back to the original pattern
    LD A,8
ME4:
    LD (IX+2),A ; store the value back
ME5:

    LD A,(IX+0) ; get current Y position
    INC A ; fixed increase for now
    CP 150
    JR C,ME3
    ; enemy has reached the bottom of the screen
    ; decrease score

    ; explosion?

    ; clear enemy data
    XOR A
    LD (HL),A
    ; clear sprite
```

```
        LD A,209
ME3:
        LD (IX+0),A
ME2:
        INC HL
        DJNZ ME1
        ; adjust our animation timing
        LD A,(ANIMATE)
        DEC A
        JP P,ME6
        LD A,4
ME6:
        LD (ANIMATE),A

        RET
```

Another bit of complicated code, so I will step through it as follows:

1. We set up a loop, so we can work through all our 20 enemy objects.
2. First, we check that an enemy object is on screen by checking that our enemy byte value is not zero.
3. Next, we need to work out the sprite memory position so we can look at and adjust the shape and position of the sprite (can you think of a way this could be made more efficient?)
4. Now we get our enemy data byte – in our example this will always be 1, so we don't use it for the moment.
5. I have included a step that changes the sprites pattern each frame, thus producing a slight animation effect.
6. Next, we move the enemy down the screen, simply by adding 1 to the Y value – another thing we can make more complex later.
7. Next, we need to detect when enemies have reached the bottom of the screen, so they can be removed.
    Later, we can add an explosion effect and sound, etc.
8. We use the DJNZ command to keep going around our loop until we have processed all the enemy objects.
9. Next, we adjust our animation byte, so we know which pattern to use next frame for our enemies.

9.3. Summary

We have covered a fair bit of ground in this chapter, now we can:

*   move our ship,
*   fire bullets

We have our 1st type of enemy being generated and moving on the screen.

Next chapter we will cover some basic collision detection, between the players bullet and the enemy objects, and show how to add scoring to our game.

10.   Collision Detection

In this chapter we are going to add some simple collision detection so that the bullets our ship is firing can hit and destroy the asteroids that are falling down the screen.

At this stage we only have one type of enemy, which is at a fixed size, but later we will have different sized asteroids as well as some other enemy types, so we need to allow for different sizes.

10.1.   Step One – Object Collisions

Our first step is to write a function that works out whether two objects of different sizes have hit each other.

Now how do we check two objects have hit each other. Well, it requires a little bit of maths, not too complicated, but very important.

In interests of simplicity, and processing time, I always treat objects on 8-bit systems as rectangles. What we are trying to do is work out whether two rectangles intersect as follows:

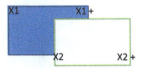

Figure 16 - Detecting the collision of two objects

So, in this example 1st step is we see our 2nd object plus its width (don't worry about X and Y at this stage, it's the same both ways, just with different values), is less than the position of the 1st object. If it is, they can't be hitting so we exit.

```
LD A,(IX+0)
SUB E
CP (IY+0)
JR NC,NOHIT
```

Next, we see if the 1st object plus its width, is less than the position of the 2nd object.

Just like the first step, if this is true, then they can't be hitting so we exit.

```
ADD A,E ; get our original value back
ADD A,L
CP (IY+0)
JR C,NOHIT
```

So, after we have done that, we have finished in one direction.

So, the remainder of the code just repeats for the other coordinate and widths.

```
LD A,(IX+1)
SUB D
CP (IY+1)
JR NC,NOHIT
ADD A,D ; get our original value back
ADD A,H
CP (IY+1)
JR C,NOHIT
```

If we make it through this section of code, the two objects have hit each other, so we set the carry flag and return.

```
    SCF
    RET
```

Otherwise, we clear the carry flag and return.

```
NOHIT:
    XOR A
    RET
```

So, our complete function is as follows:

```
; ======================================================
; Test whether two objects are colliding
; ======================================================
; IX+0 = 1st object Y
; IX+1 = 1st object X
; IY+0 = 2nd object Y
; IY+1 = 2nd object Y
; D = 2nd object width
; E = 2nd object height
; H = 1st object width
; L = 1st object height
; ======================================================
; Result: Carry flag set if two objects collide
; ======================================================
COLTST:
    LD A,(IX+0)
    SUB E
    CP (IY+0)
    JR NC,NOHIT
    ADD A,E ; get our original value back
    ADD A,L
    CP (IY+0)
    JR C,NOHIT
    LD A,(IX+1)
    SUB D
    CP (IY+1)
    JR NC,NOHIT
    ADD A,D ; get our original value back
    ADD A,H
    CP (IY+1)
    JR C,NOHIT
    SCF
    RET
NOHIT:
    XOR A
    RET
```

10.2.   Step Two – Enemy Collisions

Now let's put the new collision detection routine into use.

Inside the **MOVE_ENEMIES** function we created in the previous chapter, replace the section before the **ME2** label as follows:

```
        ; clear sprite
        LD A,209
ME3:
        LD (IX+0),A
        JR ME2
ME3:
        LD (IX+0),A

        ; enemy object has been moved now do collision detection
        LD IY,SPRTBL+8 ; bullet y position
        LD A,(IY+0)
        CP 209 ; check that it is on screen
        JR Z,ME2
        PUSH HL ; save values so we can use the registers
        PUSH DE
        LD HL,0E0Eh ; set our meteor size at 14x14
                    ; - will change per enemy type later
        LD DE,0208h ; set our bullet size at 2x8
        CALL COLTST
        POP DE
        POP HL
        JR NC,ME2
        ; we have a hit, for the moment just make both objects disappear
        LD A,209
        LD (IY+0),A
        LD (IX+0),A
        XOR A
        LD (HL),A ; deactivate the enemy
        ; later we will:
        ; - increase the score
        ; - explosion sound
        ; - animate enemy

ME2:
        INC HL
        DJNZ ME1
```

For each of our active enemy objects, this will check whether they have hit the current player bullet.

For the time being, if they do collide, both the enemy and the bullet will just be removed from the screen.

11. Scoring

In this chapter we are adding scoring to our game.

Our Megablast game is based on Astro Smash for the Intellivision and in that game, you increase your score by shooting various enemies plus lose score if any of the enemies make it to the ground.

This is another reason it makes a good example game, as we get to cover both increasing and decreasing a player's score.

So, to get started let's look at how we are going to keep track of the player's score.

To make displaying the score a bit easier we are going to use a special Z80 set of instructions that assist with Binary Coded Decimal (BCD) values.

What is BCD you ask? It is special number storage mode that instead storing the values 0-255 in each byte, it stores a single decimal digit (0-9) in each of the two nibbles (4-bits) in a byte i.e. you can store from 0-99 per byte of memory.

This does seem to be a bit of a waste, but this allows us to easily display a decimal representation of the number with very little work (as we will go through below).

In our game we are going to use three bytes of RAM to hold the player's current score.

If you always make the last digit of the score zero, this will allow us to have seven digits for scores from 10 to 99,999,990.

So, to make our scoring work we are going to need five things:

- A routine to display the current score to the screen
- A routine to add to the player's score
- A routine to subtract from the player's score
- A display routine to draw to the screen
- The routines to add and subtract points to and from the player's score at the appropriate places in our game.

11.1. Displaying the Current Score

Next, we need a routine to display our score on the screen.

But we need to store our score (and lives) somewhere, so at the end of our source file change the RAM definitions to the following:

```
;********************************************************************
; RAM Definitions
;********************************************************************

ORG RAMSTART

LEVEL:          DS 1
LIVES:          DS 1
SCORE:          DS 3
LASTSCORE:      DS 3
ENEMYDATA:      DS 20
ANIMATE:        DS 1
```

And, of course, we should make sure these new RAM definitions are cleared in our INIT_RAM function as follows:

```
; Init Ram for a new game
INITRAM:
    LD A,3
    LD (LIVES),A
    LD HL,0
    LD (SCORE),HL
    LD (SCORE+1),HL
    LD A,1
    LD (LASTSCORE),A
    XOR A
    LD (LEVEL),A
    LD (ANIMATE),A
```

Next, we need to create a DISPLAYSCORE function.

```
; Display the current score on the 2nd last row
DISPLAYSCORE:
; compare the 1st score digit with our lastscore value
LD A,(SCORE)
LD HL,LASTSCORE
CP (HL)
RET Z
```

This first part of the routine checks that the 1st digit of our score has changed, by comparing it with the value stored in LASTSCORE. This prevents us from wasting time displaying the score if our score hasn't changed.

```
; setup our write to video RAM
LD HL,VRAM_NAME + 707
CALL SETWRT
```

Next, we set the current video RAM pointer to be at position 707 (or row 22, column 3).

```
        ; starting at our last byte, write out each of the
        ; two digits per byte
        LD HL,SCORE+2
        LD B,3
SLP:
        ; output the two decimal digits currently in A
        CALL PRINTIT
        DEC HL
        DJNZ SLP
```

Here we loop through each of the three bytes for our score, calling for each one the PRINTIT subroutine that will display the two digits stored in our score value.

Basically, PRINTIT takes each nibble in the byte and adds it to our character for zero in our pattern table and outputs that value to our screen name table.

```
        ; save the current score value into lastscore
        LD A,(SCORE)
        LD (LASTSCORE),A
        RET
```

To finish up we get our current score value and store it in the LASTSCORE byte, so we don't keep on writing to the screen, if our score has not changed.

11.2.   Adding to the Current Score

Next, we need to create a routine to add to the current score. We will call this routine with the amount to add to the score in the Accumulator (A).

```
; Add A to the current score
; - Score is stored as three two-nibble decimal values.
; - Displaying a fixed zero at the end this gives a
;   score range of 7 digits, i.e. max score is 99,999,990.
SCOREADD:
    PUSH DE ; save DE
    PUSH HL ; save HL
```

First, we save the current values of the DE and HL registers on the stack as they will be changed by this routine.

This way we only have to worry about A being changed when the routine is called.

```
    ; add value in A to the current 1st score byte
    LD HL,SCORE
```

The HL register is used to point to the byte of our Score that we are working on.

```
    LD E,A
    LD A,(HL)
    ADD A,E
    ; adjust into a two nibble decimal
    DAA
    ; save to 1st score byte
    LD (HL),A
```

In this section of our code, we put our value to add into E, then get the current value of our 1st score byte, add E to it, then use the BCD command DAA, which will handle changing the value into BCD format. The carry flag will be set if the number is larger than 99.

```
    ; now add any overflow to the 2nd score byte
    INC HL
    LD A,(HL)
    ADC A,0
    DAA
    LD (HL),A
```

In this section we add one to the next score byte, if the carry flag was set from the 1st add.

```
; now add any overflow to the 3rd score byte
INC HL
LD A,(HL)
ADC A,0
DAA
LD (HL),A
```

In this section we do the same for the 3rd score byte, I probably could have used a loop for this as these two sections of code are identical. Shows how there are always multiple ways of doing things.

```
POP HL ; restore HL
POP DE ; restore DE
RET
```

Lastly, we restore our HL and DE values from the stack and return to our calling code.

11.3.   Subtracting from the Current Score

Next, we need to add a routine to subtract from the current Player's score.

This is a little bit more complicated, but it is a good example of subtraction with values larger than can be stored in a single byte of memory.

```
; Subtract A from the current score
; - Score is stored as three two nibble decimal values.
; - Displaying a fixed zero at the end this gives a
;   score range of 7 digits, i.e. max score is 99,999,990.
SCORESUB:
    PUSH DE ; save DE
    PUSH HL ; save HL
```

First, we save the values in the DE and HL registers as we will be changing them.

```
; subtract value in A from the 1st score byte
LD E,A
LD HL,SCORE
LD A,(HL)
SUB E
; adjust into a two-nibble decimal
DAA
; save to 1st score byte
LD (HL),A
```

Next, we point HL to our 1st score byte of memory and then subtract the value passed in the Accumulator (A) from it, use the DAA command to adjust it back into a BCD value and finally we store the value back into our 1st score byte.

```
; now add any overflow to the 2nd score byte
INC HL
LD A,(HL)
SBC A,0
DAA
LD (HL),A
```

Next, if we overflowed, i.e. made our 1st score byte less than zero, we need to subtract one from the 2nd score byte, adjust it back to a BCD value and store it back in the 2nd byte.

```
; now add any overflow to the 3rd score byte
INC HL
LD A,(HL)
SBC A,0
DAA
LD (HL),A
```

Next, we repeat the same code for the 3rd score byte. Once again, a loop could have been used here.

```
JR NC, SCORESUB2
; we have overflowed - set score to zero
XOR A
LD (HL),A
DEC HL
LD (HL),A
DEC HL
LD (HL),A
```

Now if we got an overflow on our 3rd byte then we have either made the score larger than 99,999,990 (unlikely, as we subtracted a number) or we have made our score negative. We don't want negative scores, so we just reset all three score bytes back to zero.

```
SCORESUB2:
     POP HL ; restore HL
     POP DE ; restore DE
     RET
```

Finally, we restore the HL and DE registers, so they are not affected by what happens inside this routine.

11.4.   Calling the Display Routine

Another thing we need to do is call the Score Display routine when we can write to the screen (and not cause graphical issues). So, the best place for that is our VDP blank routine.

The sample code already includes this call as follows:

```
; This is our routine called every VDP interrupt during normal game play
; - Do all VDP writes here to avoid corruption
VDU_WRITES:
     CALL DISPLAYSCORE
     RET
```

11.5.   Adding Scoring to our Game

Right so now we have all our routines ready, all we need to do is call our SCOREADD and SCORESUB routines at some appropriate places in our code.

So, we will subtract from the score when an enemy reaches the bottom of the screen.

In the MOVE_ENEMIES routine find the comment:

```
; decrease score
```

And after that add the following two lines:

```
LD A,1
CALL SCORESUB
```

So, this is going to decrease our effective score by 10 points every time one of the enemy objects reaches the bottom of the screen.

Next, we will increase the score when we shoot one of the enemies.

Further down in the MOVE_ENEMIES routine find the comment:

```
; later we will:
```

And replace it with the following code:

```
; increase our score for hitting the asteroid
; Note: later we will vary the score by type of enemy
LD A,2 ; 20 points per asteroid hit
CALL SCOREADD

; later we will:
; - explosion sound
; - animate enemy
```

So, each time we shoot one of the enemies we will add 20 points to the player's score.

Later, we will add on a different number of points based on the type of enemy that has been destroyed.

That's all for this episode, in the next episode we will handle the player getting killed and displaying the number of remaining lives on screen.

12.   Player Collisions and Lives

In this chapter we are going to cover two things, detecting whether any enemy objects hit the player ship and displaying the number of lives the player has remaining.

Of course, this will also include detecting when the player is out of lives and ending the game.

12.1.   Player Collisions

First, we need to see if any of the enemy objects have hit the player ship. The best place to do this is in our existing enemy object loop, located in the **MOVE_ENEMIES** subroutine.

One little fix to start in this routine, as the amount of code has increased, some of our previous relative jumps will be out of range, i.e. the jump will be too far.

Find the label ME1 and just after replace the JR Z,ME2 with the following:

```
JP  Z,ME2
```

Now find the code where we detect whether the enemy object has reached the bottom of the screen i.e.

```
; fixed increase for now
INC A
CP 150
JR C,ME3
; enemy has reached the bottom of the screen
```

Now after this code, we add a section of code to see if the enemy object has hit the player as follows:

```
; enemy has reached the bottom of the screen
; check whether the enemy has hit the player ship
LD A,(SPRTBL+1)
SUB 14 ; fixed width of enemy at the moment
CP (IX+1)
JR NC, ME7
; x + it's width is larger than the players X
ADD A,28
CP (IX+1)
JR C, ME7
; we should be hitting the player
; decrease the players life counter
LD A,(LIVES)
DEC A
; check we don't overflow
JR NC,ME9
XOR A
ME9:
LD (LIVES),A
; at the moment we won't do any animation effect
; TODO: Animate players death

; continue on so that we finish our enemy loop and subroutine
JR ME8
ME7:
; have not hit the player decrease score
```

And we need to add our label ME8 just after our decrease score section as follows:

```
; decrease score
LD A,1
CALL SCORESUB
; explosion?

ME8:
```

One more range fix, go to the bottom of our function and look for the DJNZ ME1 command just after an INC HL, replace that with a normal jump as follows:

```
ME2:
    INC HL
    DEC B
    JP NZ,ME1
```

Now, we only have one type of enemy object so we will hardwire the width to 14 pixels. As we only need to test the x direction, we do the test here in line rather than calling our collision testing function.

12.2. Display the Player's Lives

Next, we need to display the current number of player's remaining lives on the screen. Rather than display them with a number, let's be a little bit more creative and display a graphic symbol of the players ship for each life.

We need to do a couple of bits of set-up a new bit of memory. Go to the end of the main assembly file and find our memory declaration section as follows:

```
ORG RAMSTART

LEVEL:       DS 1
LIVES:       DS 1
```

Add one more line after LIVES as follows:

```
LASTLIVES:   DS 1
```

This is our indicator of what the number of lives were last time we wrote them to the screen, so we don't have to write them every frame.

As we have added a new variable, we need to set it to a known value. Find our INITRAM function and update it as follows:

```
; Init RAM for a new game
INITRAM:
    LD A,3
    LD (LIVES),A
    LD HL,0
    LD (SCORE),HL
    LD (SCORE+1),HL
    LD A,1
    LD (LASTSCORE),A
    XOR A
    LD (LASTLIVES),A
    LD (LEVEL),A
    LD (ANIMATE),A
```

Next, we need to display our lives on screen 1st with a DISPLAYLIVES function. Replace the existing one with the following code:

```
; Display the current player lives (max 7)
DISPLAYLIVES:
    LD HL,LIVES
    LD A,(LASTLIVES)
    CP (HL)
    RET Z
    ; clear current lives display
    LD HL,VRAM_NAME+688
    LD BC,14
    XOR A
    CALL FILVRM
    LD HL,VRAM_NAME+720
    LD BC,14
    XOR A
    CALL FILVRM
    ; now show the current lives
    ; - first write the top characters
```

```
        LD D,44
        LD HL,VRAM_NAME+688
        CALL SETWRT
        ; current # of lives
        LD A,(LIVES)
        ; max 7 to be displayed
        AND %111
        LD B,A
DL1:
        LD A,D
        OUT (DATA_PORT),A
        INC A
        OUT (DATA_PORT),A
        DJNZ DL1
        ; - now write the bottom characters
        LD D,42
        LD HL,VRAM_NAME+720
        CALL SETWRT
        ; current # of lives
        LD A,(LIVES)
        ; max 7 to be displayed
        AND %111
        LD B,A
DL2:
        LD A,D
        OUT (DATA_PORT),A
        INC A
        OUT (DATA_PORT),A
        DJNZ DL2
        LD A,(LIVES)
        LD (LASTLIVES),A
        RET
```

At the start of the routine, we check whether the current lives counter is different from the value in our LASTLIVES value. If it is different, we know to update the lives display.

This routine basically draws two rows, forming the top and bottom tiles of the lives counter, with two tiles per player life. It stops at a maximum of seven life counters. Otherwise, we would run out of screen space.

And of course, at the end we store the current number of lives in LASTLIVES for the next time the routine is called.

We need to display the lives at the start of the game, so just before MLOOP add the following code:

```
        CALL DISPLAYLIVES

        LD A,1
        LD (LASTSCORE),A
        CALL DISPLAYSCORE

        LD HL,VDU_WRITES
        CALL SET_VDU_HOOK
        CALL ENABLE_NMI

        ; Main game logic loop
MLOOP:
```

The final thing we need to do is call our DISPLAYLIVES routine, and the best place to do that is during our vertical blank routine, just after our DISPLAYSCORE call as follows:

```
; This is our routine called every VDP interrupt during normal game play
; - Do all VDP writes here to avoid corruption
VDU_WRITES:
        CALL DISPLAYSCORE
        CALL DISPLAYLIVES
        RET
```

12.3.   Game Over

The truly final touch is to end the game if the player's lives reach zero. This time we will simply exit back to the title screen. We will enhance this some more in a later episode.

Find our MLOOP section and just after the call to MOVE_ENEMIES we add code to detect whether the player life counter has reached zero as follows:

```
        CALL MOVE_ENEMIES

        ; test to see if we have run out of lives
        ; TODO: Display G A M E   O V E R message, wait and new game
        LD A,(LIVES)
        CP 0
        JP Z,TITLESCREEN
```

One more thing before we finish, we need to erase any remaining sprites on screen before we display the title screen. Otherwise, there will probably be sprites still on the screen. So, just after our TITLESCREEN label add the following lines to clear any sprites from the screen as follows:

```
TITLESCREEN:
        ; display our title screen
        CALL DISABLE_NMI
        ; Clear the screen
        CALL CLEARPAT

        ; Clean up in case the game left anything on screen
        CALL CLEARSPRITES
        CALL SPRWRT
```

13.   More Enemies

In this chapter we are going to enhance the generation of the enemy objects.

Currently we are only making one type of asteroid appear, whereas we want a variety of enemies to appear on screen with different movement logic and behaviour.

We won't cover all the eventual enemy types in this chapter, but we will put together the framework so we can add more in the next steps.

13.1.   Enemy Management

So, before we get started, we need to plan out our memory structures that will handle different types of enemies.

My preferred way is to work out what different things you will need for each enemy type and then make a table of the common things you need to store.

There are two tables, one to store our base information about an enemy, which will be stored in ROM and the second to store the information we need in RAM during a game session.

ROM Table

Name	Bytes	Description
Starting Shape	1	Starting Sprite Pattern
Ending Shape	1	Ending Sprite Pattern
DX	1	Any starting change in X (we will randomly choose the direction)
DY	1	Any starting change in Y
Score	1	The value added to the players score when destroyed
Width	1	The width of our enemy for collision detection
Spare	2	Round our bytes out to 8, makes are maths a little easier and you never know what you might want to add later.

In our code for our game, we would have a table as follows:

```
; Enemy source data table
; Start Shape, End Shape, DX, DY, Score
DB 12, 16, 0, 1, 10, 16 ; Large Meteor
DB 20, 24, 0, 2, 20, 10 ; Small Meteor
DB 28, 40, 1, 2, 50, 10 ; Smart Bomb
DB 44,48, 0, 0, 0, 16   ; Explosion
```

The enemy type is used as the index into the table in ROM, and knowing that each table entry is 8 bytes long we can calculate the address quite simply as follows:

```
; A contains the enemy type index
LD HL, ENEMY_TYPES
; multiply index by 8
SLA A
SLA A
SLA A
; add to our original location
LD C,A
LD B,0
ADD HL, BC
```

RAM Table

Name	Bytes	Description
Enemy Type	1	This indicates the type of our enemy object as follows: 0 – None 1 – Large Meteor 2 – Small Meteor 3 – Smart Bomb 4 – Explosion
DX	1	Our current change in X i.e. the amount to add/subtract from X to move our enemy
DY	1	Our current change in Y i.e. the amount to add/subtract from Y to move our enemy

Note:

This could be made more efficient by sharing bytes for several indicators. There are only have a handful of enemy types, so we don't really need 8 bits to store that. But there is always a trade-off in this case, both speed and readability (2nd of which is important in a tutorial like this), so we will stick with separate bytes for each of our values.

13.2. Updated Code

So, let's apply this technique to our existing code in our templates.

Set up

First, we need to add our data table. Place this near the end of the file either before or after the TITLE_SCREEN_PAT section as follows:

```
; Enemy source data table
ENEMY_TYPES:
    ; Start Shape, End Shape, DX, DY, Score, Width, Spare1, Spare2
    DB 8, 16, 0, 1, 10, 16, 0, 0 ; Large Meteor
    DB 20, 24, 0, 2, 20, 12, 0, 0 ; Small Meteor
    DB 28, 40, 1, 2, 50, 12, 0, 0 ; Smart Bomb
    DB 44, 48, 0, 0, 0, 16, 0, 0   ; Explosion
```

Also add a useful function for calculating the address in ROM of an enemy type as follows:

```
; Calculate base enemy data location in ROM
; A = enemy type (assumed to be 1 or greater)
; Returns:
; IY = Enemy Type data in ROM
CALC_ENEMY:
    ; save registers we are going to change
    PUSH AF
    PUSH HL
    PUSH DE
    LD HL,ENEMY_TYPES
    DEC A
    ; divide by 8
    SLA A
    SLA A
    SLA A
    LD E,A
    LD D,0
    ADD HL,DE
    ; set our return data
    PUSH HL
    POP IY
    ; restore registers we changed
    POP DE
    POP HL
    POP AF
    RET
```

We need to allocate more RAM for our enemy data table as follows:

```
ENEMYDATA:    DS 60
```

And cover this in our INITRAM function as follows:

```
; Init RAM for a new game
INITRAM:
     LD A,3
     LD (LIVES),A
     LD HL,0
     LD (SCORE),HL
     LD (SCORE+1),HL
     LD A,1
     LD (LASTSCORE),A
     XOR A
     LD (LASTLIVES),A
     LD (LEVEL),A
     LD (ANIMATE),A
     ; initialise enemy data
     LD HL,ENEMYDATA
     LD (HL),A
     LD DE,ENEMYDATA+1
     LD BC,59
     LDIR
     RET
```

Spawn Enemies

We need to update our SPAWN_ENEMIES section of code to cater for the extra RAM positions and storing our DX and DY values as follows:

```
; Spawn/create new enemies
SPAWN_ENEMIES:
     LD A,(LEVEL)
     INC A
     SLA A ; multiply by 4
     SLA A
     LD C,A
     CALL RND
     CP C
     RET NC
     ; see if there is an enemy object available
     LD HL,ENEMYDATA
     LD B,20
SE1:
     XOR A
     CP (HL)
     JR NZ,SE2
     ; enemy available
     PUSH HL
     ; calc our sprite memory position
     LD A,20
     SUB B
     SLA A
     SLA A
     LD C,A
     LD B,0
     LD HL,SPRTBL+12
     ADD HL,BC
     ; set Y to zero
     LD A,0
     LD (HL),A
     ; set X to a random value
```

```
        INC HL
        CALL RND
        LD (HL),A
        ; set pattern
        INC HL
        LD A,8
        LD (HL),A
        ; set colour
        INC HL
        LD A,0dh
        LD (HL),A
        POP HL
        ; hard wire to enemy type 1 for now
        LD A,1
        CALL CALC_ENEMY
        LD (HL),A
        INC HL
        LD A,(IY+2) ; DX
        LD (HL),A
        INC HL
        LD A,(IY+3) ; DY
        LD (HL),A
        RET
SE2:
        ; move to the next data position (now 3 RAM spaces per enemy)
        INC HL
        INC HL
        INC HL
        ; dec b and jump if non-zero
        DJNZ SE1
        RET
```

Move Enemies

We need to update our MOVE_ENEMIES section of code as follows:

```
; Move any active enemies
MOVE_ENEMIES:
    LD HL,ENEMYDATA
    LD B,20
ME1:
    XOR A
    CP (HL)
    JP Z,ME2
    ; found active enemy
    ; calc our sprite memory position (20-B) * 4
    PUSH BC
    LD A,20
    SUB B
    SLA A
    SLA A
    LD C,A
    LD B,0
    LD IX,SPRTBL+12
    ADD IX,BC
    POP BC
    ; get our enemy data
    LD A,(HL)
    ; get the pointer to our enemy data
    CALL CALC_ENEMY

    LD A,(ANIMATE)
    CP 0
    JR NZ,ME5
    ; animate our sprite pattern (hardwired for the moment)
    LD A,(IX+2) ; get current pattern
    ADD A,4      ; add four
    CP (IY+1)    ; compare against our ending pattern
    JR NZ,ME4    ; if we have reached our ending pattern
                 ; we need to move back to the original pattern
    LD A,(IY+0) ; starting sprite shape
ME4:
    LD (IX+2),A ; store the value back
ME5:
    ; get current Y position
    LD E,(IX+0)
    ; change Y at the rate defined in the enemy RAM data table
    INC HL
    INC HL
    LD A,(HL)
    DEC HL
    DEC HL
    ADD A,E
    CP 150
    JR C,ME3
    ; enemy has reached the bottom of the screen
    ; check whether the enemy has hit the player ship
    LD A,(SPRTBL+1)
    SUB A,(IY+5) ; width of enemy from enemy data table
    CP (IX+1)
    JR NC, ME7
    ; x + it's width is larger than the players X
    LD A,(SPRTBL+1)
```

```
        ADD A,(IY+5)
        CP (IX+1)
        JR C, ME7
        ; we should be hitting the player
        ; decrease the players life counter
        LD A,(LIVES)
        DEC A
        ; check we don't overflow
        JR NC,ME9
        XOR A
ME9:
        LD (LIVES),A
        ; at the moment we won't do any animation effect
        ; TODO: Animate players death

        ; continue on so that we finish our enemy loop and subroutine
        JR ME8
ME7:
        ; have not hit the player decrease score
        ; decrease score
        LD A,1
        CALL SCORESUB
        ; explosion?

ME8:
        ; clear enemy data
        XOR A
        LD (HL),A
        ; clear sprite
        LD A,209
        LD (IX+0),A
        JR ME2
ME3:
        LD (IX+0),A

        ; enemy object has been moved now do collision detection
        LD A,(SPRTBL+8) ; bullet y position
        CP 209 ; check that it is on screen
        JR Z,ME2
        PUSH HL ; save values so we can use the registers
        PUSH DE
        PUSH IY
        LD A,(IY+5) ; get our width
        LD L,A
        LD H,L
        LD IY,SPRTBL+8
        LD DE,0208h ; set our bullet size at 2x8
        CALL COLTST
        POP IY
        POP DE
        POP HL
        JR NC,ME2
        ; we have a hit, for the moment just make both objects disappear
        LD A,209
        LD (SPRTBL+8),A
        LD (IX+0),A
        XOR A
        LD (HL),A ; de-activate the enemy
        ; increase our score for hitting the asteroid
        ; Vary the score by type of enemy
        LD A,(IY+4) ; get our points from the enemy data table
```

```
        CALL SCOREADD

        ; later we will:
        ; - explosion sound
        ; - animate enemy

ME2:
        INC HL
        INC HL
        INC HL
        DEC B
        JP NZ,ME1
        ; adjust our animation timing
        LD A,(ANIMATE)
        DEC A
        JP P,ME6
        LD A,2
ME6:
        LD (ANIMATE),A

        RET
```

14. TMS9928A/TMS9929A - Graphics

In this chapter we are going to cover some more technical details on how the graphics are handled on ColecoVision, this information can also apply to these additional systems that use the same graphics chip:

- MSX
- Spectravideo
- Sega SG-1000/SC-3000
- TI-99/4A
- Memotech MTX
- Creativision (Dick Smith Wizzard)
- Einstein
- Sord M5
- NABU

Each of these systems have a main processor (all bar one uses a Z80A CPU) with their own RAM, but this processor does not handle anything to do with creating output on the screen i.e. graphics.

To do that all these systems have a 2nd CPU from Texas Instruments called the TMS9928A (NTSC – TMS9929A for PAL systems).

The TMS processor has its own RAM area, often called VRAM (for Video RAM). Key points to understand how this works are:

- The TMS Processor has direct access only to its own RAM, and
- Likewise, the Z80 only has direct access to its RAM

So, unlike other machines, like the Commodore 64 and Spectrum you can't just write a value to a memory location and have it change what happens on the screen.

That is, for your code to control what is happening on the screen, the TMS processor has several ports (think of them as serving windows) that you use to send information to or receive information from the Video RAM.

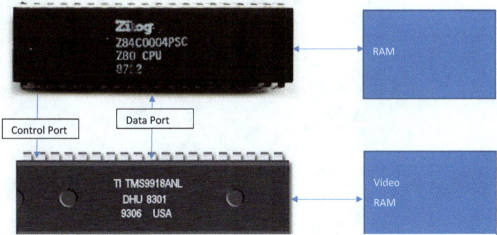

Figure 17 - Relationship between the Z80 CPU and the TMS Graphics Processor

This may seem strange, especially to programmers of other systems, but it is modelled on how a lot of arcade games were created, with different processors controlling different things, like video and sound.

The advantages of this are:

- The main processor, the Z80, does not have to do anything to draw the screen for each frame.
- The main processor does not have to share its RAM with anything, so there is no delay in accessing the RAM at any stage.
- The Video RAM is completely dedicated to the TMS processor, and being 16K, with reasonably high resolution (for 8-bit standards), colour, and of course 32 hardware sprites, it is capable of very faithful recreations of early arcade games.

The disadvantages of this are:

- There are limits to how fast information can be sent to or read from Video RAM using the ports to the TMS processor. So, you can't change large amounts of Video RAM for each frame.
- Therefore, smooth scrolling can be difficult to achieve on TMS-based systems.

14.1.   Video RAM Break Down

The TMS processor has several different modes available as follows:

Graphics Modes I & II

These two modes have a screen resolution of 256 x 192 pixels, broken up into 8 x 8-pixel tiles, i.e. 32 x 24 or 768 tiles.

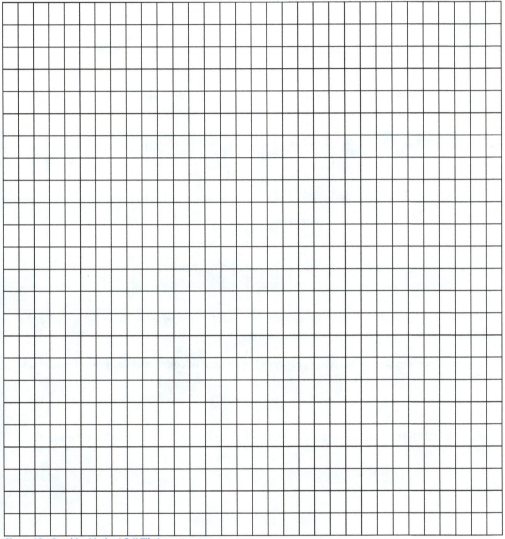

Figure 18 - Graphics Modes I & II Tile Layout

Each tile has 8 bytes of RAM that define the pattern or shape as follows:

```
00011000
00111100
01111110
11011011
11111111
00100100
01011010
10100101
```

Both Mode I and Mode II have 768 tile patterns so each tile pattern can be unique.

But how each mode handles colour is different as follows.

- Mode I groups each of the tile patterns into blocks of 8, each of these blocks has the same foreground and background colour.

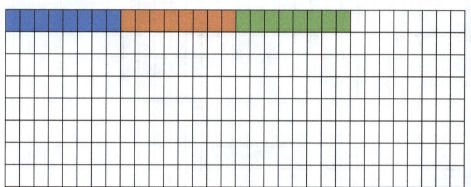

- Mode II has another 8 bytes for each pattern. Each of the bytes describe the foreground and background colour for a row of the pattern.

The two modes seem similar but differ greatly in the amount of colour and pattern detail that can be displayed.

Mode I harks back to when memory was more expensive, and if the TMS chip was only supplied with 4K of Video RAM.

Mode II uses 12k just for the patterns and colour information, it needs more to hold the pattern positions and sprite table.

Both modes support the 32 hardware sprites.

Text Mode

Text Mode is just that. Designed purely to display text, it can display 40 columns across 24 rows, a total of 960 tiles. The patterns for each of the tiles come from a table of 256 patterns.

Each tile has 8 bytes of RAM that define the shape, but only the least significant 6 bits (the right 6 bits) define the pattern, e.g.:

```
XX001100
XX010010
XX010010
XX100001
XX111111
XX100001
XX100001
XX100001
```

The positions marked with an X are ignored.

There is only a single foreground and background colour for the whole screen and sprites are not available in this mode.

Multicolour Mode

The Multicolour Mode is quite different from the other modes in that it allows unrestricted use of the 16 available colours but at a much lower resolution of 64 x 48 pixels.

Sprites are also available in this mode.

14.2.   Hardware Sprites

In all modes (other than text mode), 32 hardware sprites are available, these sit in front of the graphics/background layer.

All sprites can be either 8x8 or 16x16 pixels in size and can be displayed as "double size" where the pixels are doubled in size.

Each sprite can be any one of the 15 colours. Multi-coloured images are created by stacking multiple sprites on top of each other.

There can be a maximum of four sprites displayed in a row on the screen, but with clever coding up to eight in a row can be achieved with minor flickering.

These hardware sprites, along with the high resolution of the background tiles, are what allow TMS systems to emulate early 80's arcade games so well.

We'll have a more in depth look at sprites in the next chapter.

14.3.   Example Code – TMS Demo

For this chapter, we will not advance the game we have been working on but instead look at some examples of what the TMS graphics chip can do with a demo.

In our demo directory we put our base template, along with a set of tile patterns to get us started.

Compiling and running this starting template in our emulator will get you a simple start-up screen with a title as follows:

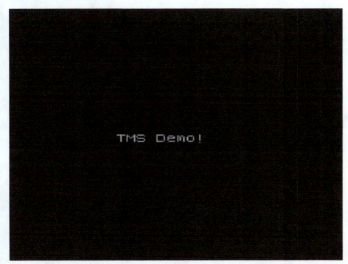

Let's add some things to our template, nothing fancy, just a couple of items that will help visualise how the TMS chip uses its video memory to draw the display and some simple techniques to add some nice visual effects.

Animating a tile pattern

The top 256 tile positions of our screen we set to be the same pattern (in this case tile pattern 69).

Add this section of code after the label TITLESCREEN: and after the highlighted text below:

```
; now setup our initial screen layout
; top 1/3 of the screen
LD HL,VRAM_NAME
LD BC,256
LD A,69
CALL FILVRM
```

That's not that interesting. So, let's introduce some animation, adding this code to our interrupt routine:

```
; This is our routine called every VDP interrupt during the title screen
; - Do all VDP writes here to avoid corruption
OUTPUT_VDP_TITLE:
    ; do our pattern and colour animations
    LD A,(WAIT)
    CP 0
    JR Z, OVT1
    DEC A
    LD (WAIT),A
    RET
OVT1:
    LD A,8
    LD (WAIT),A
    ; 1. animate the pattern in tile 69
    LD HL,69*8
    CALL SETWRT
    LD B,4
    LD A,(LASTPATTERN1)
LP1:
    OUT (DATA_PORT),A
    OUT (DATA_PORT),A
    XOR 0ffh
    DJNZ LP1
    XOR 0ffh
    LD (LASTPATTERN1),A
    RET
```

We need to reserve two bytes of RAM for our counter and last pattern storage:

```
ORG RAMSTART

WAIT: ds 1
LASTPATTERN1: ds 1
```

And it's always good to initialise it to a known value when we start as follows in our INITRAM function:

```
; Initialise any RAM we will be using
INITRAM:
    LD A,204
    LD (LASTPATTERN1),A
    LD A,8
    LD (WAIT),A
    RET
```

This will change the pattern being displayed for our tile and thus change all 256 positions at one time. Assemble it and give it a go.

You don't have to work with only a single pattern. With a bit of planning, you can get quite a nice, detailed animation going with more tiles, e.g., 4 tiles arranged 2 x 2.

Animating the colour table

For the middle 256 tile positions of our screen, I used tile pattern 70, which has changing bands of colour (different shades of red) running down it. Plus, I added a border around our text using tile pattern 72 as follows:

```
; middle 1/3 of the screen
LD HL,VRAM_NAME + 256
LD BC,256
LD A,70
CALL FILVRM

; our initial text
LD HL,VRAM_NAME + 32*12 + 10
CALL SETRD
LD HL,TITLE_TEXT
CALL OUTPUT_TEXT

; add a box of characters around the text
LD HL,VRAM_NAME + 256 + 32*2 + 6
LD BC,20
LD A,72
CALL FILVRM
LD HL,VRAM_NAME + 256 + 32*3 + 6
CALL SETWRT
LD A,72
OUT (DATA_PORT),A
LD HL,VRAM_NAME + 256 + 32*3 + 25
CALL SETWRT
LD A,72
OUT (DATA_PORT),A
LD HL,VRAM_NAME + 256 + 32*4 + 6
CALL SETWRT
LD A,72
OUT (DATA_PORT),A
LD HL,VRAM_NAME + 256 + 32*4 + 25
CALL SETWRT
LD A,72
OUT (DATA_PORT),A
LD HL,VRAM_NAME + 256 + 32*5 + 6
CALL SETWRT
LD A,72
OUT (DATA_PORT),A
```

```
LD HL,VRAM_NAME + 256 + 32*5 + 25
CALL SETWRT
LD A,72
OUT (DATA_PORT),A
LD HL,VRAM_NAME + 256 + 32*6 + 6
LD BC,20
LD A,72
CALL FILVRM
```

It not only looks nice, but it also shows the higher resolution colour abilities of the TMS chip.

Now, even though that doesn't look too bad, let's jazz it up by animating the colour bands for tile pattern 70, by adding code to our interrupt routine before the RET statement as follows:

```
; 2. animate the palette entries on the 2nd zone
LD HL,VRAM_COLOR + 0800h + 70 * 8
CALL SETWRT
LD A,(LASTPATTERN2)
INC A
CP 3
JR NZ,OVT2
XOR A
OVT2:
LD (LASTPATTERN2),A
LD HL,COLOURTABLE
LD C,A
LD B,0
XOR A
ADC HL,BC
LD A,(HL)
OUT (DATA_PORT),A
OUT (DATA_PORT),A
OUT (DATA_PORT),A
INC HL
LD A,(HL)
OUT (DATA_PORT),A
OUT (DATA_PORT),A
OUT (DATA_PORT),A
INC HL
LD A,(HL)
OUT (DATA_PORT),A
OUT (DATA_PORT),A
RET
```

Just below that add a little bit of data that will control which colours we will cycle through as follows:

```
COLOURTABLE:
DB 096,128,144,096,128
```

We need to reserve a byte of RAM for our counter:

```
ORG RAMSTART

WAIT: ds 1
LASTPATTERN1: ds 1
LASTPATTERN2: ds 1
```

And once again initialise it to a known value in our INITRAM function:

```
INITRAM:
    LD A,204
    LD (LASTPATTERN1),A
    XOR A
    LD (LASTPATTERN2),A
```

More colour table animation

For the last 256 tile positions of our screen, I used tile pattern 71, which has vertical bands as follows:

```
; last 1/3 of the screen
LD HL,VRAM_NAME + 512
LD BC,256
LD A,71
CALL FILVRM
```

Let's add one more piece of code to our interrupt routine as follows:

```
; 3. animate the palette entries in the 3rd zone
LD A,(LASTPATTERN3)
; swap upper and lower number by rotating 4 times
RLCA
RLCA
RLCA
RLCA
LD (LASTPATTERN3),A
LD HL,VRAM_COLOR + 01000h + 71*8
LD BC,8
CALL FILVRM
RET
```

We need to reserve a byte of RAM for our counter:

```
ORG RAMSTART

WAIT: ds 1
LASTPATTERN1: ds 1
LASTPATTERN2: ds 1
LASTPATTERN3: ds 1
```

And once again initialise it to a known value in our INITRAM function:

```
LD A,045h
LD (LASTPATTERN3),A
```

So, by swapping the two colours the tile uses we can introduce an animation, that makes it look like that section of the screen is scrolling (although depending on how your eyes see it, it will be either going left to right or right to left ☺).

Finally, we have a very simple demo showing off some techniques that can jazz up your games on TMS systems.

In our next part we will have a proper look at how the TMS processor handles sprites.

15. TMS9928A/TMS9929A - Sprites

In this chapter we continue from the last chapter where we looked at how the TMS99XXA graphics chip displays tile graphics, making a bit of a graphical demo in the process.

In addition to the character tiles the TMS processor allows 32 sprites to be displayed on top of the background.

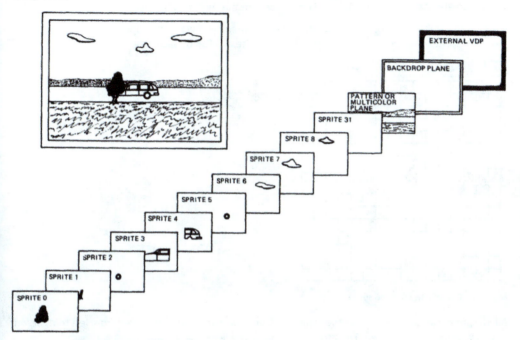

Figure 19 - TMS9928A/TMS9929A Sprite Display Order

The sprites can be in one of four modes:

- 8x8 pixels
- 16x16 pixels
- 8x8 pixels magnified
- 16x16 pixels magnified

This mode applies to all sprites in use, i.e., you cannot mix and match.

Each sprite can be set to one of the 15 available colours, if you want the appearance of, multi-coloured sprites then you need to place multiple sprites on top of each other e.g.

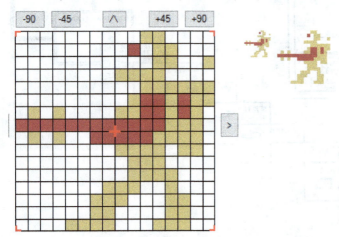

Figure 20 - Example two layered sprite

All 32 sprites can be on screen at the same time, but only the 1st four displayed from left to right, on any row, will show on screen. The fifth sprite on a row will not be drawn.

This will cause some of your sprites to disappear or flicker as they move past other sprites.

The example libraries that have been supplied already include code to allow up to 8 sprites per line; by changing the order the sprites are drawn each alternate frame.

The human eye will not even notice the minor flickering this introduces; so, this works quite well.

But there is still an upper limit of eight sprites in a row, so you need to take this into account when designing your games.

15.1.   Using Sprites

TMS Sprites are quite easy to use, each of the 32 sprites is controlled using four bytes of video RAM (called the sprite control table) as follows:

Byte 1 – sprite Y position (0-255)

Byte 2 – sprite X position (0-255)

Byte 3 – sprite pattern number (0-255)

Byte 4 – sprite colour (0-15)

Rather than having to deal with reading and writing the sprite control table in Video RAM, I like to have a copy of the table in normal Z80 RAM and copy it to Video RAM each vertical blank.

This simplifies your code greatly, as you don't have to worry about when you can change a sprite value.

With the supplied routines it also automatically allows 8 sprites per line by reversing the draw order of the sprites every 2nd frame as part of the routine to update Video RAM.

To make a sprite disappear from the screen set its Y coordinate to 209.

15.2. On With Our Demo

Now let's extend the graphics demo from the last chapter and have all 32 sprites on screen moving around so that we can see this in effect.

Sprite shapes

We are going to use 16x16 sprites for our demo and I have included four shape designs as follows:

We need to add these to our file ending with "-Patterns.asm", you can either cut and paste the code below or use the Sprite Editor to output the file from the supplied "TMSDemo.spr" file.

```
SPRITE_1:
    ; Sprite sprite_1 pattern 1
    db 003,012,016,042,074,064,186,147
    db 146,146,082,064,042,026,012,003
    db 192,048,008,164,170,002,077,209
    db 073,069,090,002,172,168,048,192
SPRITE_2:
    ; Sprite sprite_1 pattern 1
    db 003,012,016,037,085,064,164,189
    db 164,164,101,064,053,021,012,003
    db 192,048,008,084,082,002,209,017
    db 145,065,146,002,084,088,048,192
SPRITE_3:
    ; Sprite sprite_1 pattern 1
    db 003,012,016,042,074,064,154,162
    db 146,136,114,064,042,026,012,003
    db 192,048,008,164,170,002,117,039
    db 037,037,038,002,172,168,048,192
SPRITE_4:
    ; Sprite sprite_1 pattern 1
    db 003,012,016,037,085,064,167,162
    db 162,130,098,064,053,021,012,003
    db 192,048,008,084,082,002,073,121
    db 073,073,074,002,084,072,048,192
```

Loading Sprite Patterns

Next, we need to load the sprite pattern data into Video RAM so that we can use them in our sprites.

```
; Send the sprite definitions to the VDP
LOAD_SPRITES:
    LD HL,VRAM_SPRGEN
    LD DE,SPRITE_1
    LD BC,32*SPRITECOUNT
    CALL LDIRVM
    RET
```

The TMS processor allows us to have 256 8x8 patterns that can be used for our sprites.

When we use 16x16 sprites though, each sprite needs four patterns that are one after each other, as you can only specify the pattern number of the 1st pattern.

The TMS processor then assumes the other three patterns are the next three patterns after the one you specify.

In our main code file, we need to update the SPRITECOUNT value to equal the number of sprite patterns we have i.e. 4

```
SPRITECOUNT: EQU 4
```

And of course, we need to call the new routine above, which we might as well do just after we load the character tiles as follows:

```
; Load the character set, make all three sections the same
CALL LOAD_CHR_SET
; Load our sprite patterns
CALL LOAD_SPRITES
```

Draw Our Sprites

Next, we need to put our sprites on screen. So, to start with let's display all 32 of them in a rough circle on the screen.

The easiest way to do this is to have a set of data and copy it to our sprite table. So, add the following data section to our main code file:

```
; Place our sprites on screen
PLACE_SPRITES:
    LD HL,SPRITE_PLACEMENT
    LD DE,SPRTBL
    LD BC,32*4
    LDIR
    RET

; Sprite placement data
SPRITE_PLACEMENT:
    db 096,048,0,01
    db 080,056,0,02
    db 064,064,0,03
    db 048,072,0,04
    db 040,088,0,05
    db 032,104,0,06
    db 024,120,0,07
```

```
db 032,136,0,08
db 040,152,0,09
db 048,168,0,10
db 064,176,0,11
db 080,184,0,12
db 096,192,0,13
db 110,184,0,14
db 124,176,0,15
db 140,168,0,01
db 148,152,0,02
db 156,136,0,03
db 164,120,0,04
db 156,104,0,05
db 148,088,0,06
db 140,072,0,07
db 124,064,0,08
db 110,056,0,09
db 096,048,0,10
db 172,056,0,11
db 172,104,0,12
db 172,136,0,13
db 172,184,0,14
db 008,056,0,15
db 008,120,0,01
db 008,184,0,02
```

And after the CALL LOAD_SPRITES command above add a call to the placement routine as follows:

```
; place the sprites on the screen in their initial positions
CALL PLACE_SPRITES
```

Build the code and run in the emulator and you should get something like this:

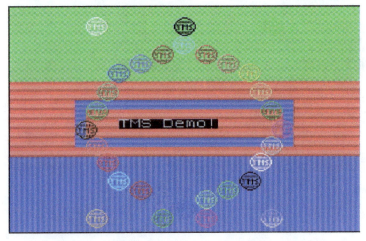

Figure 21 - TMS Demo Running

Animate Our Sprites

Now, let's make things a bit more interesting and animate our sprites by cycling them through a few different patterns a couple of times a second.

This is also a good example of how to use the timing code included in the sample templates.

In our template we have a section of code that will be executed two times a second, add the following code there, but change it from the HalfSecTimer to the QtySecTimer since we want our change to happen four times a second instead of two:

```
SPLASH_TITLE2:
    LD  A,(QtrSecTimer)
    CALL  TEST_SIGNAL
    OR  A
    JR  Z,  SPLASH_TITLE2

    ; animate our sprite shapes
    LD  HL,ANIMATION_TABLE
    LD  B,0
    LD  A,(ANIMATION_STEP)
    LD  C,A
    ADC  HL,BC
    LD  A,(HL)
    CP  255
    JR  NZ,UL1
    ; we have reached the end of our animation table
    XOR  A
    LD  (ANIMATION_STEP),A
    LD  A,(ANIMATION_TABLE)
UL1:
    LD  HL,SPRTBL+2
    LD  B,32
UL2:
    LD  (HL),A
    INC  HL
    INC  HL
    INC  HL
    INC  HL
    DJNZ  UL2

    ; increment our animation step
    LD  HL,ANIMATION_STEP
    INC  (HL)

    JR  SPLASH_TITLE2

ANIMATION_TABLE:
    DB  0,4,8,12,255
```

We need to declare the bit of RAM we are using for our ANIMATION_STEP variable as follows:

```
ORG RAMSTART

WAIT: ds 1
LASTPATTERN1: ds 1
LASTPATTERN2: ds 1
LASTPATTERN3: ds 1
ANIMATION_STEP: ds 1
```

And we must always remember to initialise any variables to a known value in our **INITRAM** function as follows:

```
INITRAM:
    LD A,204
    LD (LASTPATTERN1),A
    XOR A
    LD (LASTPATTERN2),A
    LD (ANIMATION_STEP),A
```

Build the ROM and give it a go in the emulator, you should now see our sprites animating.

Move Our Sprites

To finish off let's make the sprites move around the screen. For simplicity, we will make each sprite move in a random direction.

Now we need to add a data table to hold each of our sprite X & Y velocities, i.e., how much they are going to move and which way.

So, add a new RAM space (after ORG RAMSTART) as follows:

```
SPRITE_VELOCITY: DS 64
```

Now let's add a function to set our random X & Y velocities as follows:

```
; Set our sprite velocities
SET_VELOCITY:
     LD HL,SPRITE_VELOCITY
     LD B,32
SV1:
     CALL RND
     LD C,A
     AND %00000111
     INC A
     BIT 7,C
     LD (HL),A
     JR Z,SV2
     LD A,255
     SUB (HL)
     LD (HL),A
SV2:
     INC HL
     CALL RND
     AND %00000111
     INC A
     BIT 7,C
     LD (HL),A
     JR Z,SV3
     LD A,255
     SUB (HL)
     LD (HL),A
SV3:
     INC HL
     DJNZ SV1
     RET
```

Call this new routine, just after the CALL PLACE_SPRITES we added earlier as follows:

```
CALL PLACE_SPRITES
CALL SET_VELOCITY
```

Now let's add a function to move the sprites based on their current velocity:

```
; Move our sprites based in their velocity
MOVE_SPRITES:
    LD HL,SPRTBL
    LD DE,SPRITE_VELOCITY
    LD B,32
MS1:
    LD A,(DE)
    LD C,A
    LD A,(HL)
    ADD A,C
    LD (HL),A
    INC HL
    INC DE
    LD A,(DE)
    LD C,A
    LD A,(HL)
    ADD A,C
    LD (HL),A
    INC HL
    INC DE
    INC HL
    INC HL
    DJNZ MS1
    RET
```

And we call it just after our animation code from above as follows:

```
    LD HL,ANIMATION_STEP
    INC (HL)

    CALL MOVE_SPRITES

    JR SPLASH_TITLE2
```

If you build and run that you should see all 32 sprites moving in different directions and speeds.

You can play around with the original placement data and try modifying the code that sets the velocities to get different movement patterns.

That's all for this chapter.

Next, we start covering sound, so we can add sound effects to our game.

16.   Generating Sounds

In this chapter, we are going to look at how we generate sound. This will allow us to add sound effects for our game, e.g., our laser shooting, explosions when things are destroyed etc.

16.1.   SN76489A Sound Chip

The ColecoVision (as well as the TI-99/4A, Sega SG-1000/SC-3000 and Memotech MTX) uses a Texas Instruments SN76489A Programmable Sound Generator chip that has 3 tone generators and 1 noise generator.

The SN76489A can only generate square waves, but you can control the tone and volume of each of the four channels.

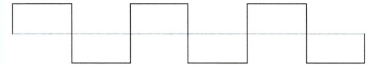

22 - SN76489A output wave shape

The frequency of each tone channel has 10 bits - values from 0 to 1023. 1 is the highest frequency (111861Hz) and 1023 is the lowest frequency (109Hz).

This gives a frequency range of 8 octaves from A2 – 10 cents, to A12 – 12 cents.

The noise channel can either generate periodic or white noise with two bits remaining, that set a shift rate.

The volume of each channel has 4 bits - values from 0 to 15. Zero represents full volume, and 15 represents silence.

This can be a lot to absorb. So, before we get too carried away, let's learn by using some code that will allow us to play with the tone and volume of each channel.

So, first, we add some code to initialise the sound chip to a known state as follows:

```
; ***********************************************************
; Sound routines
; ***********************************************************
SOUND_PORT: EQU 0FFh   ; SN76489A

; Initialise the sound chip, so that no sound is playing
INIT_SOUND:
  LD A,%10011111       ; Tone 1 volume =  off
  OUT (SOUND_PORT), A
  LD A,%10111111       ; Tone 2 volume =  off
  OUT (SOUND_PORT), A
  LD A,%11011111       ; Tone 3 volume =  off
  OUT (SOUND_PORT), A
  LD A,%11111111       ; Noise volume =  off
  OUT (SOUND_PORT), A
  RET
```

As you can see there is only one port for the ColecoVision's sound chip, and when setting the volume of a channel you only need to output a single byte.

Our next section of code is a single routine that will set the volume of all three tone channels and the noise channel from stored values in RAM as follows:

```
; sets the current volume of each of the sound channels
SET_SOUND_VOLUME:
  LD HL,CH1VOL
  LD A,%10010000 ; Channel 1 volume
  OR (HL)
  OUT (SOUND_PORT),A
  INC HL
  LD A,%10110000 ; Channel 2 volume
  OR (HL)
  OUT (SOUND_PORT),A
  INC HL
  LD A,%11010000 ; Channel 3 volume
  OR (HL)
  OUT (SOUND_PORT),A
  INC HL
  LD A,%11110000 ; Noise volume
  OR (HL)
  OUT (SOUND_PORT),A
  RET
```

Next, we need a routine to set the current frequency of each channel from the 10-bit value stored in our RAM area.

```
SET_ALL_SOUND_FREQUENCIES:
  LD HL,CH1FRQ
  LD D,%10000000
  CALL SET_SOUND_FREQUENCY
  LD D,%10100000
  CALL SET_SOUND_FREQUENCY
  LD D,%11000000
  CALL SET_SOUND_FREQUENCY
  RET

SET_SOUND_FREQUENCY:
  LD A,(HL)
  AND 00Fh
  OR D
  OUT (SOUND_PORT),A
  LD A,(HL)
  AND 0F0h
  LD D,A
  INC HL
  LD A,(HL)
  AND 00Fh
  OR D
  RRCA
  RRCA
  RRCA
  RRCA
  OUT (SOUND_PORT),A
  INC HL
  RET
```

So, these two routines, allow all channels to be updated from our RAM values. The 2nd routine handles sending the channel select along with the upper bits of the frequency as well as the 2nd byte of data containing the lower bits of the frequency.

All the code above can just be typed in or copied and pasted into the template, just before the **LOAD_CHR_SET** code is a good spot.

16.2. Sound Example

The code provided with this chapter has the usual Start and End folders.

The Start folder contains a template application, that sets up the system and loads some tiles to display some text on the screen.

This example application will allow us to play with the sound chips tone and volume levels for each channel, using our joystick controller.

The code to move a sprite pointer between each of the channel's tone and volume settings is already included. When you run the application, it should look like this:

Figure 23 - Sound Effect Demo

You should be able to increase and decrease the volume of the current channel by pressing up or down on the joystick. Pressing left or right will decrease or increase the frequency of the current channel. Pressing the fire button will move the pointer to the next channel.

Now, add the code from earlier in this document. It can be added just before the LOAD_CHR_SET routine.

Now, let's add code to call each of these routines.

Right near the start of our code, find where we "initialise clock" and add the following call to **INIT_SOUND**.

```
CALL INIT_SOUND

; initialise clock
LD   HL,TIMER_TABLE
LD   DE,TIMER_DATA_BLOCK
CALL INIT_TIMER
```

Next, find the comment "set cursor position" and insert the following code, to set some initial values, before it:

```
LD A,12
LD (CH1VOL),A

CALL SET_ALL_SOUND_FREQUENCIES
CALL SET_SOUND_VOLUME

; set cursor position
```

Now our starting code already changes the volume and frequency values in RAM. So, we just need to call our routines to send them to the sound processor as follows:

```
CALL  SELECT_CHANNEL
CALL  PLAYER_ACTIONS
CALL  SET_ALL_SOUND_FREQUENCIES
CALL  SET_SOUND_VOLUME

JR SPLASH_TITLE2
```

This code will increase or decrease the currently selected Tone or Volume value and then update the sound chip to be the same value.

When you run the application, it should look the same. But now if you move the joystick up and down on a field you should hear a continuous sound being output.

So, we have covered a lot of concepts in this episode, and probably what seems like only a small amount of code, but hopefully something interesting to play with.

Next chapter we will generate some actual sound effects for our game.

17. Sound Effects

Last chapter we learnt how to create sounds using the ColecoVision's sound chip. Now let's use the OS 7 BIOS functions to add some sound effects to our game, Mega Blast.

We have a simple game. So, we can limit the sounds to our major game actions as follows:

- Player shooting – a nice laser zap sound
- Player laser hitting an enemy – a small explosion sound
- Enemy hitting player – a big explosion sound
- Enemy reaching the ground – another small explosion sound

The ColecoVision's sound chip can only generate square waves. So, to create some simple sound effects, we will need to change the frequency being output over a period of time.

To help create sound effects a tool that allows you to draw the shape of the sound effect you want to generate. It outputs the values that can be sent to the OS 7 BIOS functions.

The tool is Coleco Sound Effects, written in Java, and should work on most platforms with Java installed.

I have made an adjusted version of the tool supporting the assemblers used in this book, download a copy of the tool here:

https://www.electricadventures.net/Content/PGFTC/cvsoundfx.zip

This tool only outputs simple, noise, or end notes (See SIMPLE NOTE, NOISE and END OR REPEAT).

The adjusted source code can be found here in the book GitHub repository here:

https://github.com/tony-cruise/ProgrammingGamesForTheColeco

I am working on a new version of the Sprite and Tile Editor that will also allow you to 'draw' sound effects, like this application and allow you to use more of the OS 7 sound routine features. Keep checking my website for more details on this in the future.

17.1.   OS 7 BIOS Sound

The ColecoVision (and Adam) have functions built in for playing sound (and music).

The functions work on a standard set of data divided into two sections.

- Sounds Effects and Music Data
- Sound Address Table

Sounds Effects and Music Data

The OS 7 functions can generate a range of different sound effects and notes.

The following information is the sound data format for the songs encoded in ColecoVision games.

Channel # (2-bit values):

00 = Noise, 01 = Tone 1 Generator, 10 = Tone 2 Generator, 11 = Tone 3 Generator.

A noisy sound needs a specific sound data format. Numbers 7 to 0 indicate its position.

Volume Values

The volume for a sound is controlled through a coarse 4-bit volume value, allowing volume levels from 0 to 28 dB as follows:

A3	A2	A1	A0	Weight
0	0	0	0	2 dB
0	0	0	1	4 dB
0	1	0	0	8 dB
1	0	0	0	16 dB
1	1	1	1	OFF

The are 9 different sound data formats that can be used.

REST

Silences the specified tone generator for the period specified.

7	6	5	4	3	2	1	0
Channel #		1	Length				

SIMPLE NOTE

Plays a tone at a fixed frequency and volume on a single tone generator for the specified length.

7	6	5	4	3	2	1	0
Channel #		0	0	0	0	0	0
Frequency (8 lower bits)							
Volume in 4 bits				0	0	Frequency (2 hi-bits)	
Length							

FREQUENCY SWEPT NOTE

Plays a tone that sweeps up or down, from a starting frequency at a fixed volume on a single tone generator. The change in the frequency is controlled by the number of steps, the step size, and the length of time for each step. The length of the 1st step can be different from the following ones.

7	6	5	4	3	2	1	0
Channel #		0	0	0	0	0	1
Frequency (8 lower bits)							
Volume in 4 bits				0	0	Frequency (2 hi-bits)	
Number of steps in a sweep							
Step Length				1st step length			
Step size							

VOLUME SWEPT NOTE

Plays a tone that plays a fixed frequency note from a starting volume and then sweeps the volume up or down on a single-tone generator. The change in the volume is controlled by the number of steps, the step size and the length of time for each step. The length of the 1st step can be different from the following ones.

7	6	5	4	3	2	1	0
Channel #		0	0	0	0	1	0
Frequency (8 lower bits)							
Volume in 4 bits				0	0	Frequency (2 hi-bits)	
Number of steps in a sweep							
Step size				Number of steps			
Step length				1st step length			

VOLUME AND FREQUENCY SWEPT NOTE

Plays a tone on a single-tone generator starting at a specified frequency and volume. It then sweeps both the frequency and volume. The change in both the volume and frequency is controlled by the number of steps, the step size, and the length of time for each step. The length of the 1st step can be different from the following ones.

7	6	5	4	3	2	1	0
Channel #		0	0	0	0	1	1
Frequency (8 lower bits)							
Volume in 4 bits				0	0	Frequency (2 hi-bits)	
Number of steps in a sweep							
Frequency step length				1st frequency step length			
Frequency step size							
Volume step				Number of volume steps			
Volume step length				1st volume step length			

NOISE

Plays either Period (buzzing sound) or White (shhh or hissing sound) noise. The variation in the frequency of the noise can be controlled by a set Shift Rate or by linking it to the frequency of the 3rd tone generator.

7	6	5	4	3	2	1	0
0	0	0	0	0	0	1	0
Unused byte (0)							
Volume in 4 bits				0	FB	NF1	NF0
Length of note							

FB = 0 Period Noise (buzz), 1 White Noise (shhh)

NF1/NF0 = Shift Rate, 0/0 N/512, 0/1 N/1024, 1/0 N/2048 or 1/1 controlled by tone generator 3

NOISE VOLUME SWEEP

Plays either Period (buzzing sound) or White (shhh or hissing sound) noise. The variation in the frequency of the noise can be controlled by a set Shift Rate or by linking it to the frequency of the 3rd tone generator.

The volume will sweep up or down, controlled by the size, number, and length of the steps. The length of the 1st step can be different from the following steps.

7	6	5	4	3	2	1	0
0	0	0	0	0	0	1	0
Initial volume				0	FB	NF1	NF0
Length of note							
Step size				Number of volume step			
Step length				1st volume step length			

FB = 0 Period Noise (buzz), 1 White Noise (shhh)

NF1/NF0 = Shift Rate, 0/0 N/512, 0/1 N/1024, 1/0 N/2048 or 1/1 controlled by tone generator 3

SPECIAL EFFECT

This causes the OS 7 routine to call a function of your own making. Be sure to preserve all registers before returning (RET) to the calling routine.

7	6	5	4	3	2	1	0
Channel #		0	0	0	1	0	0
Address of the special effect sub-routine (in 2 bytes of course)							

END OR REPEAT

Use as the last part of any sound data set, to either signal the end of the routine or to repeat the routine. The sound will repeat until the sound buffer is re-used for another sound.

7	6	5	4	3	2	1	0
Channel #		0	1	Repeat 0/1	0	0	0

Sound Address Table

The Sound Address Table defines all the sounds effects and music pieces you are going to use, and which of the playing buffers that a sound will use.

You can reuse the same buffer between sounds, but which-ever sound is played last will take over that sound buffer.

If you start a sound sequence that repeats, it will repeat indefinitely until another sound sequence is started on the same buffer.

Our final table for this section will look as follows (overwrite the same section in the source code):

```
SoundDataCount:       EQU 7
Len_SoundDataArea:    EQU 10*SoundDataCount+1 ; 7 data areas
SoundAddrs:
 DW sfx_ZAP1_1,SoundDataArea        ; 1 Laser zap sound (Channel 1)
 DW sfx_EXPLOSION1_0,SoundDataArea+10 ; 2 Explosion 1 part 1 (Noise)
 DW sfx_EXPLOSION1_3,SoundDataArea+20 ; 3 Explosion 1 part 2 (Channel 3)
 DW sfx_EXPLOSION2_0,SoundDataArea+10 ; 4 Explosion 2 part 1 (Noise)
 DW sfx_EXPLOSION2_3,SoundDataArea+20 ; 5 Explosion 2 part 2 (Channel 3)
 DW sfx_EXPLOSION3_0,SoundDataArea+30 ; 6 Explosion 3 part 1 (Noise)
 DW sfx_EXPLOSION3_3,SoundDataArea+40 ; 7 Explosion 3 part 2 (Channel 3)
 DW  0,0
```

17.2. Player Shooting

So, for our first sound using the Coleco Sound Effects tool, draw a descending line.

Note: Make sure you remove any red parts to the right of where your line ends.

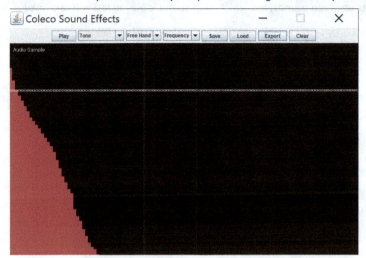

Figure 24 - A nice zap sound using the Coleco Sound Effects program

Press the [Export] button and a form will pop up as follows:

Figure 25 - Coleco Sound Effects - Select Channel

It is asking which of the three tone channels you want the sound effect to use, select [Tone Channel 1] and then it will pop-up another form as follows:

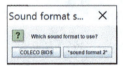

Figure 26 - Coleco Sound Effects - Select Sound Format

Press the [COLECO BIOS] button and another form will pop-up as follows:

Figure 27- Coleco Sound Effects - Select Assembly Code

Press the [Assembly code (SDCC)] button and the next pop-up will ask for a label, I have chosen ZAP1 as the label here:

Figure 28 - Coleco Sound Effects - Add a label

And the next form will ask you for a filename to save the data to.

I used ZAP.s as my filename, here is what the program output:

```
;    .globl   sfx_ZAP1_1

sfx_ZAP1_1:
      DB $40,$77,$30,1
      DB $40,$b3,$30,1
      DB $40,$e1,$30,1
      DB $40,$fb,$30,1
      DB $40,$13,$31,1
      DB $40,$2d,$31,1
      DB $40,$45,$31,1
      DB $40,$65,$31,1
      DB $40,$75,$31,1
      DB $40,$87,$31,1
      DB $40,$99,$31,1
      DB $40,$b1,$31,1
      DB $40,$c5,$31,1
      DB $40,$d9,$31,1
      DB $40,$ed,$31,1
      DB $40,$09,$32,1
      DB $40,$2f,$32,1
      DB $40,$57,$32,1
      DB $40,$7d,$32,1
      DB $40,$9b,$32,1
      DB $40,$bb,$32,1
      DB $40,$cf,$32,1
      DB $40,$1b,$33,1
      DB $40,$3d,$33,1
      DB $40,$53,$33,1
      DB $40,$7b,$33,1
      DB $40,$9b,$33,1
      DB $40,$bb,$33,1
      DB $40,$cf,$33,1
      DB $40,$db,$33,1
      DB $40,$f5,$33,1
      DB $40,$fb,$33,1
      DB $50
```

Another way to achieve a similar zap sound using a single Frequency Swept Note instead of the Simple Note. This set of data will generate a changing waveform.

```
sfx_ZAP1_1:
      DB $41,$77,$30,$10,$11,$20
      DB $50
```

This uses the same channel, starting at the same frequency and volume as the previous sound, but increasing in frequency over 16 steps. All from a single set of data values.

17.3.   Player Laser Hitting an Enemy

To make an explosion sound we need to use the noise sound channel.

There are two different types of noise to choose from: Periodic and White noise.

For an explosion, White Noise usually works best. So, for a short explosion a waveform like this should do:

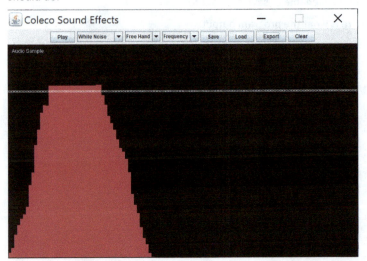

After output, I shortened the 1st section to 30, and then removed lines from the 2nd part (sfx_EXPLOSION1_3) until the numbers in the last column added up to 30, leaving the last data line:

```
sfx_EXPLOSION1_0:
    DB $00,$00,$37,30
    DB $10
sfx_EXPLOSION1_3:
    DB $c0,$e7,$f3,1
    DB $c0,$d1,$f3,1
    DB $c0,$91,$f3,1
    DB $c0,$63,$f3,1
    DB $c0,$45,$f3,1
    DB $c0,$2f,$f3,1
    DB $c0,$0b,$f3,1
    DB $c0,$a3,$f2,1
    DB $c0,$67,$f2,1
    DB $c0,$e3,$f1,1
    DB $c0,$99,$f1,1
    DB $c0,$49,$f1,1
    DB $c0,$25,$f1,1
    DB $c0,$27,$f1,1
    DB $c0,$c7,$f0,16
    DB $d0
```

17.4. Enemy Hitting Player

For an enemy hitting the player, we want a bit bigger explosion. So, more than one frequency peak, once again, mixed with some white noise should give a suitable sound.

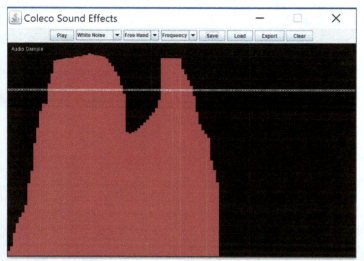

After output, doing the fix steps, and removing the 2nd last data item you end up with:

```
sfx_EXPLOSION2_0:
    DB $00,$00,$37,120
    DB $10
sfx_EXPLOSION2_3:
    DB $c0,$e7,$f3,1
    DB $c0,$d1,$f3,1
    DB $c0,$91,$f3,1
    DB $c0,$63,$f3,1
    DB $c0,$45,$f3,1
    DB $c0,$2f,$f3,1
    DB $c0,$0b,$f3,1
    DB $c0,$a3,$f2,1
    DB $c0,$67,$f2,1
    DB $c0,$e3,$f1,1
    DB $c0,$99,$f1,1
    DB $c0,$49,$f1,1
    DB $c0,$25,$f1,1
    DB $c0,$27,$f1,1
    DB $c0,$c5,$f0,1
    DB $c0,$95,$f0,1
    DB $c0,$57,$f0,1
    DB $c0,$53,$f0,1
    DB $c0,$51,$f0,1
    DB $c0,$4f,$f0,1
    DB $c0,$4b,$f0,3
    DB $c0,$45,$f0,1
    DB $c0,$43,$f0,2
    DB $c0,$3d,$f0,2
    DB $c0,$35,$f0,1
    DB $c0,$39,$f0,1
    DB $c0,$3d,$f0,1
    DB $c0,$3f,$f0,1
    DB $c0,$41,$f0,1
```

```
DB  $c0,$45,$f0,1
DB  $c0,$4d,$f0,1
DB  $c0,$61,$f0,1
DB  $c0,$71,$f0,1
DB  $c0,$8b,$f0,1
DB  $c0,$a1,$f0,1
DB  $c0,$cd,$f0,1
DB  $c0,$f5,$f0,1
DB  $c0,$ad,$f1,1
DB  $c0,$b3,$f1,1
DB  $c0,$ad,$f1,1
DB  $c0,$a7,$f1,1
DB  $c0,$9b,$f1,1
DB  $c0,$8d,$f1,1
DB  $c0,$7f,$f1,1
DB  $c0,$71,$f1,1
DB  $c0,$5f,$f1,1
DB  $c0,$4f,$f1,1
DB  $c0,$39,$f1,1
DB  $c0,$13,$f1,1
DB  $c0,$4b,$f0,7
DB  $c0,$7f,$f0,1
DB  $c0,$97,$f0,1
DB  $c0,$b3,$f0,1
DB  $c0,$cf,$f0,1
DB  $c0,$ff,$f0,1
DB  $c0,$4b,$f1,1
DB  $c0,$87,$f1,1
DB  $c0,$a3,$f1,1
DB  $c0,$b5,$f1,1
DB  $c0,$c7,$f1,1
DB  $c0,$33,$f2,1
DB  $c0,$61,$f2,1
DB  $c0,$9b,$f2,1
DB  $d0
```

17.5. Enemy Hitting the Ground

I am trying for an explosion sound with a bit more low-frequency rumble for hitting the ground with this waveform.

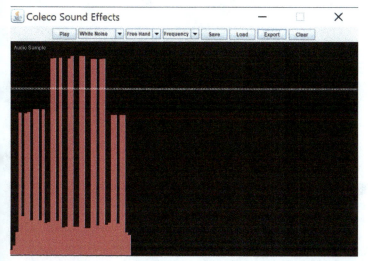

After doing the fixes, removing the end sections and adjusting the length of the noise the data looks like this:

```
sfx_EXPLOSION3_0:
    DB  $00,$00,$37,42
    DB  $10
sfx_EXPLOSION3_3:
    DB  $c0,$e7,$f3,1
    DB  $c0,$d1,$f3,1
    DB  $c0,$91,$f3,1
    DB  $c0,$55,$f1,1
    DB  $c0,$45,$f3,1
    DB  $c0,$59,$f1,1
    DB  $c0,$53,$f1,1
    DB  $c0,$59,$f3,1
    DB  $c0,$45,$f1,2
    DB  $c0,$59,$f3,1
    DB  $c0,$45,$f1,1
    DB  $c0,$65,$f3,1
    DB  $c0,$61,$f3,1
    DB  $c0,$53,$f0,1
    DB  $c0,$51,$f0,1
    DB  $c0,$5b,$f3,1
    DB  $c0,$4f,$f0,1
    DB  $c0,$7b,$f3,1
    DB  $c0,$77,$f3,1
    DB  $c0,$53,$f0,1
    DB  $c0,$47,$f0,1
    DB  $c0,$77,$f3,2
    DB  $c0,$47,$f0,2
    DB  $c0,$7d,$f3,2
    DB  $c0,$55,$f0,2
    DB  $c0,$71,$f3,1
    DB  $c0,$55,$f0,1
    DB  $c0,$53,$f0,1
```

```
DB $c0,$6d,$f3,1
DB $c0,$63,$f3,1
DB $c0,$5f,$f1,2
DB $c0,$67,$f3,1
DB $c0,$5f,$f1,2
DB $c0,$91,$f3,1
DB $c0,$9d,$f3,1
DB $d0
```

17.6.   Adding the Sound Effects to our Game

Now, we need to add the sound data we have created to our game, MegaBlast.

Carrying on from our code in Chapter 16 - More Enemies, copy the three sound effect data sets into our code file. I usually put the sound data above the Sound Address Table.

Then, copy in the Sound Address Table listed earlier in this chapter.

Make sure the game still compiles and runs in the debugger.

No sound will be generated yet, as we still need to add the commands to start each of the sounds at the appropriate time in the game.

Adding Player Shooting Sound

First, find the **FIRE_PLAYER_BULLET** function and add two lines of code to trigger the first sound as follows:

```
; Check for player bullet firing
FIRE_PLAYER_BULLET:
    ; make sure there is not already a bullet
    LD A, (SPRTBL+8)
    CP 209
    RET NZ
    ; see if the fire button is pressed
    CALL JOYTST
    CP 0
    RET Z
    ; fire bullet
    ; set Y based on player ship
    LD A, (SPRTBL)
    SUB 6
    LD (SPRTBL+8),A
    ; set X based on player ship
    LD A, (SPRTBL+1)
    ADD A,6
    LD (SPRTBL+9),A
    ; set bullet sprite pattern
    LD A,24
    LD (SPRTBL+10),A
    ; set bullet colour
    LD A,11
    LD (SPRTBL+11),A
    ; play Zap sound
    LD B,1
    CALL PLAY_IT
    RET
```

Adding Enemy Object Destroyed Sound

The next sound to add is the sound for when the player's laser hits an enemy object.

Find the **MOVE_ENEMIES** function and the comment for explosion sound just before the **ME2** label.

```
        ; later we will:
        ; - explosion sound
        ; - animate enemy

ME2:
```

Replace it with the following code:

```
        ; later we will:
        ; - animate enemy

        ; Play explosion sound
        PUSH HL    ; save the registers we are using
        PUSH BC
        LD B,2     ; queue the noise part of the sound
        CALL PLAY_IT
        LD B,3     ; queue the tone part of the sound
        CALL PLAY_IT
        POP BC     ; restore our registers
        POP HL

ME2:
```

Adding Player Ship Destroyed Sound

Next, we add the larger explosion sound for when the player's ship gets hit by an enemy object.

Find the **MOVE_ENEMIES** function and the section of code after the **ME9** label.

```
ME9:
      LD (LIVES),A
      ; at the moment we won't do any animation effect
      ; TODO: Animate players death

      ; continue on so that we finish our enemy loop and subroutine
      JR ME8
```

Replace it with the following code:

```
ME9:
      LD (LIVES),A
      ; Play our player death explosion
      PUSH HL
      PUSH IX
      PUSH BC
      LD B,4
      CALL PLAY_IT
      LD B,5
      CALL PLAY_IT
      POP BC
      POP IX
      POP HL
      ; at the moment we won't do any animation effect
      ; TODO: Animate players death

      ; continue on so that we finish our enemy loop and subroutine
      JR ME8
```

Adding Enemy Object Hitting Planet Surface Sound

The last sound we will add will be the rumbling explosion when an enemy object hits the planet's surface.

Find the **MOVE_ENEMIES** function and the comment for explosion just before the **ME8** label.

```
; decrease score
LD A,1
CALL SCORESUB
; explosion?

ME8:
```

Replace it with the following code:

```
; decrease score
LD A,1
CALL SCORESUB
; explosion?
PUSH HL ; save the registers we are using
PUSH IX
PUSH BC
LD B,6  ; play noise portion
CALL PLAY_IT
LD B,7  ; play tone portion
CALL PLAY_IT
POP BC ; restore our registers
POP IX
POP HL

ME8:
```

Compile the final code and run in the emulator and all the sounds should be working.

18. Playing Music

Now, it's time to make our system sing, well play some simple music at least.

Once again, we are going to focus on using the OS 7 Bios sound routines, but this time to play a sequence of notes that will form a piece of music.

18.1. Converting Notes to Frequencies

The easiest way to play some music is to take a written piece of music and convert the notes into frequency values using a table like the following:

	Hz	Hex	Hz	Hex	Hz	Hex	Hz	Hex	Hz	Hex
A	110.00	3F8	220.00	1FC	440.00	0FE	880.00	07F	1760.0	03F
A#/Bb	116.54	3BF	233.08	1DF	466.16	0EF	932.33	077	1864.6	03B
B	123.47	389	246.94	1C4	493.88	0E2	987.77	071	1975.5	038
C	130.81	356	261.63	1AB	523.25	0D5	1046.5	06A	2093.0	035
C#/Db	138.59	327	277.18	193	554.36	0C9	1108.7	064	2217.5	032
D	146.83	2F9	293.66	17C	587.33	0BE	1174.7	05F	2349.3	02F
D#/Eb	155.56	2CE	311.13	167	622.25	0B3	1244.5	059	2489.0	02C
E	164.81	2A6	329.63	153	659.25	0A9	1318.5	054	2637.0	02A
F	174.61	280	349.23	140	698.46	0A0	1396.9	050	2793.8	028
F#/Gb	185.00	25C	370.00	12E	739.99	097	1480.0	04B	2960.0	025
G	196.00	23A	391.99	11D	783.99	08E	1568.0	047	3136.0	023
G#/Ab	207.65	21A	416.30	10D	830.61	086	1661.2	043	3322.4	021

Note: The higher the frequency, the lower is the corresponding hex value.

https://www.simplifyingtheory.com/how-to-read-sheet-music-for-beginners/

18.2.   Play a Tune

The best way to show how to play music on the ColecoVision is to use an example.

For our purposes here I have chosen the opening riff from 'Smooth Criminal' by Michael Jackson[1].

Figure 29 - Smooth Criminal by Michael Jackson Sheet Music

The tune has two tracks, the main tune is the top track, so let's have a look at how to play that first.

Here is the data to represent the opening riff using simple notes (see SIMPLE NOTE):

```
lyrics1:
        ; ch 1, rest 30
        db   0x7e
        ; ch 1, note A2 $1fc 220Hz, Vol 4db, length 7
        db   0x40,0xfc,0x11,0x07
        ; ch 1, rest 1
        db   0x61
        ; ch 1, note A2 $1fc 220Hz, Vol 4db, length 8
        db   0x40,0xfc,0x11,0x08
        ; ch 1, rest 1
        db   0x61
        ; ch 1, note A2 $1fc 220Hz, Vol 4db, Length 7
        db   0x40,0xfc,0x11,0x07
        ; ch 1, rest 1
```

---

[1] The encoding of this tune is thanks to the hard work of Amy Purple.

```
db   0x61
; ch 1, note A2 $1fc 220Hz, Vol 4db, Length 8
db   0x40,0xfc,0x11,0x08
; ch 1, rest 1
db   0x61
; ch 1, note G1 $23b 196Hz, Vol 4db, Length 7
db   0x40,0x3b,0x12,0x07
; ch 1, rest 1
db   0x61
; ch 1, note A2 $1fc 220Hz, Vol 4db, Length 8
db   0x40,0xfc,0x11,0x08
; ch 1, rest 1
db   0x61
; ch 1, note B2 $1c5 246Hz, Vol 4db, length 15
db   0x40,0xc5,0x11,0x0f
; ch 1, rest 1
db   0x61
; ch 1, note B2 $1c5 246Hz, Vol 4db, length 30
db   0x40,0xc5,0x11,0x1e
; ch 1, rest 1
db   0x61
; ch 1, note A2 $1fc 220Hz, Vol 4db, length 7
db   0x40,0xfc,0x11,0x07
; ch 1, rest 1
db   0x61
; ch 1, note B2 $1c5 246Hz, Vol 4db, length 8
db   0x40,0xc5,0x11,0x08
; ch 1, rest 1
db   0x61
; ch 1, note C2 $1ab 261Hz, Vol 4db, length 15
db   0x40,0xab,0x11,0x0f
; ch 1, rest 1
db   0x61
; ch 1, note C2 $1ab 261Hz, Vol 4db, length 30
db   0x40,0xab,0x11,0x1e
; ch 1, rest 1
db   0x61
; ch 1, note B2 $1c5 246Hz, Vol 4db, length 7
db   0x40,0xc5,0x11,0x07
; ch 1, rest 1
db   0x61
; ch 1, note C2 $1ab 261Hz, Vol 4db, length 8
db   0x40,0xab,0x11,0x08
; ch 1, rest 1
db   0x61
; ch 1, note B2 $1c5 246Hz, Vol 4db, length 15
db   0x40,0xc5,0x11,0x0f
; ch 1, rest 1
db   0x61
; ch 1, note G1 $23b 196Hz, Vol 4db, length 15
db   0x40,0x3b,0x12,0x0f
; ch 1, rest 15
db   0x6f
; ch 1, repeat
db   0x58
```

Insert the above code just above the 'Sound settings' comment and add to the end of the **SoundAddrs** table as follows:

```
DW sfx_EXPLOSION3_3,SoundDataArea+40 ; 7 Explosion 3 part 2 (Channel 3)
DW lyrics1,SoundDataArea+50          ; 8 Smooth Criminal
DW 0,0
```

Next, we need to play the tune, so find the SPLASH_TITLE2: label and add the call to PLAY_IT just before as follows:

```
        LD B,8
        CALL PLAY_IT
SPLASH_TITLE2:
```

Assemble the code and run it in an emulator and you should hear the opening riff to Smooth Criminal, that constantly repeats.

The music will continue to play in the background while you play the game.

It does sound like the riff we want, but it lacks any character.

18.3.   Improving the Tune

The trouble with using the Simple Note structure is that the tones that are being played, are flat wave forms.

If I had not added the 'rest' commands (0x61) after each note, many of the notes would have blended into a single long note.

So how can we improve this? Well, the next set of data contains the same notes, but each note sweeps (changes) the volume of the note from low to high over the same period (see VOLUME SWEPT NOTE).

As the notes have a waveform, we also do not need the rest commands in between each note as follows:

```
lyrics1a:
    ; ch 1, rest 30
    db   0x7e
    ; ch 1, vol swept note A2 $1fc 220Hz, Vol 4db, 7 x (1 x 8), 1/1
    db   0x42,0xfc,0x11,0x07,0x18,0x11
    ; ch 1, vol swept note A2 $1fc 220Hz, Vol 4db, 8 x (1 x 8), 1/1
    db   0x42,0xfc,0x11,0x08,0x18,0x11
    ; ch 1, vol swept note A2 $1fc 220Hz, Vol 4db, 7 x (1 x 8), 1/1
    db   0x42,0xfc,0x11,0x07,0x18,0x11
    ; ch 1, vol swept note A2 $1fc 220Hz, Vol 4db, 8 x (1 x 8), 1/1
    db   0x42,0xfc,0x11,0x08,0x18,0x11
    ; ch 1, vol swept note G1 $23b 196Hz, Vol 4db, 7 x (1 x 8), 1/1
    db   0x42,0x3b,0x12,0x07,0x18,0x11
    ; ch 1, vol swept note A2 $1fc 220Hz, Vol 4db, 8 x (1 x 8), 1/1
    db   0x42,0xfc,0x11,0x08,0x18,0x11
    ; ch 1, vol swept note B2 $1c5 246Hz, Vol 4db, 15 x (1 x 14), 1/1
    db   0x42,0xc5,0x11,0x0f,0x1e,0x11
    ; ch 1, vol swept note B2 $1c5 246Hz, Vol 4db, 30 x (1 x 14), 1/1
    db   0x42,0xc5,0x11,0x1e,0x1e,0x11
    ; ch 1, vol swept note A2 $1fc 220Hz, Vol 4db, 7 x (1 x 8), 1/1
    db   0x42,0xfc,0x11,0x07,0x18,0x11
    ; ch 1, vol swept note B2 $1c5 246Hz, Vol 4db, 8 x (1 x 8), 1/1
    db   0x42,0xc5,0x11,0x08,0x18,0x11
    ; ch 1, vol swept note C2 $1ab 261Hz, Vol 4db, 15 x (1 x 14), 1/1
    db   0x42,0xab,0x11,0x0f,0x1e,0x11
    ; ch 1, vol swept note C2 $1ab 261Hz, Vol 4db, 30 x (1 x 14), 1/1
    db   0x42,0xab,0x11,0x1e,0x1e,0x11
    ; ch 1, vol swept note B2 $1c5 246Hz, Vol 4db, 7 x (1 x 8), 1/1
    db   0x42,0xc5,0x11,0x07,0x18,0x11
    ; ch 1, vol swept note C2 $1ab 261Hz, Vol 4db, 8 x (1 x 8), 1/1
    db   0x42,0xab,0x11,0x08,0x18,0x11
    ; ch 1, vol swept note B2 $1c5 246Hz, Vol 4db, 15 x (1 x 14), 1/1
    db   0x42,0xc5,0x11,0x0f,0x1e,0x11
    ; ch 1, vol swept note G1 $23b 196Hz, Vol 4db, 15 x (1 x 14), 1/1
    db   0x42,0x3b,0x12,0x0f,0x1e,0x11
    ; ch 1, rest 15
    db   0x6f
    ; ch 1, repeat
    db   0x58
```

Insert the above code just above the 'Sound settings' comment and add to the end of the **SoundAddrs** table as follows:

```
DW sfx_EXPLOSION3_3,SoundDataArea+40 ; 7 Explosion 3 part 2 (Channel 3)
DW lyrics1,SoundDataArea+50          ; 8 Smooth Criminal
DW lyrics1a,SoundDataArea+50         ; 9 Smooth Criminal (Better)
DW 0,0
```

Now change the tune number in our call to PLAY_IT, just before the SPLASH_TITLE2: label as follows:

```
        LD B,9
        CALL PLAY_IT
SPLASH_TITLE2:
```

Assemble the code and run it in an emulator and you should hear the opening riff to Smooth Criminal, that constantly repeats, but this time the notes are a more interesting, making the music more enjoyable.

18.4. Adding the 2nd Track

To improve the music even further, we need to add the notes from the 2nd track (the bass track) on the score.

This involves using the Noise channel, mixed with Channel 3, so we can control the shape of the waveform again.

Here is the data needed, insert it before or after the previous music data.

```
bass1a:
    ; ch 3, note G#3 $088, 0db, length 45
    db   0xc0,0x88,0xf0,0x2d
    ; ch 3, note G#5 $022, 0db, length 15
    db   0xc0,0x22,0xf0,0x0f
    ; ch 3, note F#3 $098, 0db, length 7
    db   0xc0,0x98,0xf0,0x07
    ; ch 3, note G#3 $088, 0db, length 8
    db   0xc0,0x88,0xf0,0x08
    ; ch 3, note A#4 $079, 0db, length 30
    db   0xc0,0x79,0xf0,0x1e
    ; ch 3, note G#5 $022, 0db, length 15
    db   0xc0,0x22,0xf0,0x0f
    ; ch 3, note G#3 $088, 0db, length 7
    db   0xc0,0x88,0xf0,0x07
    ; ch 3, note A#4 $079, 0db, length 8
    db   0xc0,0x79,0xf0,0x08
    ; ch 3, note B4 $072, 0db, length 30
    db   0xc0,0x72,0xf0,0x1e
    ; ch 3, note G#5 $022, 0db, length 15
    db   0xc0,0x22,0xf0,0x0f
    ; ch 3, note A#4 $079, 0db, length 7
    db   0xc0,0x79,0xf0,0x07
    ; ch 3, note B4 $072, 0db, length 8
    db   0xc0,0x72,0xf0,0x08
    ; ch 3, note A#4 $079, 0db, length 15
    db   0xc0,0x79,0xf0,0x0f
    ; ch 3, note F#3 $098, 0db, length 15
    db   0xc0,0x98,0xf0,0x0f
    ; ch 3, note G#5 $022, 0db, length 15
    db   0xc0,0x22,0xf0,0x0f
    ; ch 3, repeat
    db   0xd8
bass1b:
    ; period noise, vol sweep, ch3, length 15 (1 x 15), 1/2
    db   0x02,0x03,0x0f,0x1f,0x12
    ; noise, rest 14
    db   0x2f
    ; period noise, vol sweep, ch3, length 15 (1 x 15), 1/2
    db   0x02,0x03,0x0f,0x1f,0x12
    ; white noise, vol sweep, ch3, length 15 (1 x 15), 1/2
    db   0x02,0x07,0x0f,0x1f,0x12
    ; period noise, vol sweep, ch3, length 7 (1 x 15), 1/2
    db   0x02,0x03,0x07,0x1f,0x12
    ; period noise, vol sweep, ch3, length 8 (1 x 15), 1/2
    db   0x02,0x03,0x08,0x1f,0x12
    ; period noise, vol sweep, ch3, length 15 (1 x 15), 1/2
    db   0x02,0x03,0x0f,0x1f,0x12
    ; period noise, vol sweep, ch3, length 15 (1 x 15), 1/2
    db   0x02,0x03,0x0f,0x1f,0x12
    ; white noise, vol sweep, ch3, length 15 (1 x 15), 1/2
```

```
db   0x02,0x07,0x0f,0x1f,0x12
; period noise, vol sweep, ch3, length 7 (1 x 15), 1/2
db   0x02,0x03,0x07,0x1f,0x12
; period noise, vol sweep, ch3, length 8 (1 x 15), 1/2
db   0x02,0x03,0x08,0x1f,0x12
; period noise, vol sweep, ch3, length 15 (1 x 15), 1/2
db   0x02,0x03,0x0f,0x1f,0x12
; period noise, vol sweep, ch3, length 15 (1 x 15), 1/2
db   0x02,0x03,0x0f,0x1f,0x12
; white noise, vol sweep, ch3, length 15 (1 x 15), 1/2
db   0x02,0x07,0x0f,0x1f,0x12
; period noise, vol sweep, ch3, length 7 (1 x 15), 1/2
db   0x02,0x03,0x07,0x1f,0x12
; period noise, vol sweep, ch3, length 8 (1 x 15), 1/2
db   0x02,0x03,0x08,0x1f,0x12
; period noise, vol sweep, ch3, length 15 (1 x 15), 1/2
db   0x02,0x03,0x0f,0x1f,0x12
; period noise, vol sweep, ch3, length 15 (1 x 15), 1/2
db   0x02,0x03,0x0f,0x1f,0x12
; white noise, vol sweep, ch3, length 15 (1 x 15), 1/2
db   0x02,0x07,0x0f,0x1f,0x12
; noise, repeat
db   0x18
```

It is split into two sections, the first part controls the tone for channel three using simple notes, and the second part controls the noise that will be mixed with the channel three tones and sweeps the volume to make each note more defined.

We need to extend the **SoundAddrs** table as follows:

```
SoundDataCount:     EQU 8
Len_SoundDataArea: EQU 10*SoundDataCount+1 ;7 data areas
SoundAddrs:
 DW sfx_ZAP1_1,SoundDataArea           ; 1 lazer zap sound (Channel 1)
 DW sfx_EXPLOSION1_0,SoundDataArea+10  ; 2 Explosion 1 part 1 (Noise)
 DW sfx_EXPLOSION1_3,SoundDataArea+20  ; 3 Explosion 1 part 2 (Channel 3)
 DW sfx_EXPLOSION2_0,SoundDataArea+10  ; 4 Explosion 2 part 1 (Noise)
 DW sfx_EXPLOSION2_3,SoundDataArea+20  ; 5 Explosion 2 part 2 (Channel 3)
 DW sfx_EXPLOSION3_0,SoundDataArea+30  ; 6 Explosion 3 part 1 (Noise)
 DW sfx_EXPLOSION3_3,SoundDataArea+40  ; 7 Explosion 3 part 2 (Channel 3)
 DW lyrics1,SoundDataArea+50           ; 8 Smooth Criminal
 DW lyrics1a,SoundDataArea+50          ; 9 Smooth Criminal (Better)
 DW bass1a,SoundDataArea+60            ; 10 Smooth Criminal - Base Tone
 DW bass1b,SoundDataArea+70            ; 11 Smooth Criminal - Base Noise
 DW 0,0
```

I had to increase the number of sound buffers by to eight, so that all three sets of music data can be played simultaneously, along with our existing sound effects.

Now, to play the enhanced version of the tune with the bass track we need to add two more calls to PLAY_IT, just before the SPLASH_TITLE2: label as follows:

```
      ; play our music
      LD B,9
      CALL PLAY_IT
      LD B,10
      CALL PLAY_IT
      LD B,11
      CALL PLAY_IT
SPLASH_TITLE2:
```

Assemble the code and run it in an emulator and you should hear the opening riff to Smooth Criminal, that constantly repeats, but now we have both the main track and the bass track playing at the same time. It makes the whole tune a much better representation of the original music.

18.5.   Stopping the Music

One more thing to add, now that the music uses the noise channel, we don't want it to continue playing when we start the game, so we need to stop it once the user presses the fire button on the title screen.

There are two ways to do that, the first is to re-initialise the OS 7 sound libraries as follows:

```
NGAME:
    ; stop all music
    LD B,SoundDataCount
    LD HL,SoundAddrs
    CALL SOUND_INIT

    CALL DISABLE_NMI
    CALL INITRAM
```

The second way is to have another tune setup that specifically uses the buffer of an existing tune, so in our case we would need three as follows:

```
stopch1:
    db 0x50

stopch3:
    db 0xD0

stopnoise:
    db 0x10
```

Add this in the same section where the other sound/music data are.

Then extend the SoundAddrs table as follows:

```
DW  bass1b,SoundDataArea+70      ; 11 Smooth Criminal - Base Noise
DW  stopch1,SoundDataArea+50     ; 12 stop channel 1
DW  stopch3,SoundDataArea+60     ; 13 stop channel 3
DW  stopnoise,SoundDataArea+70   ; 14 stop noise channel
DW  0,0
```

And finally, add the following calls to PLAY_IT after the NGAME: label as follows:

```
NGAME:
    ; stop all music
    LD B,12
    CALL PLAY_IT
    LD B,13
    CALL PLAY_IT
    LD B,14
    CALL PLAY_IT

    CALL DISABLE_NMI
    CALL INITRAM
```

Assemble the code and run it in an emulator and you should hear the opening riff to Smooth Criminal, that constantly repeats on the title screen. When you press a trigger to start a game the music should stop, and the sound effects will work in the game.

19.   Where to from here

Now obviously our game, Mega Blast, is still quite simple and could do with several features added to turn it into a more polished and professional title.

19.1.   More Enemies

We covered extending the information we stored on each enemy object in the chapter More Enemies.

Next it would be good to add some more enemies with slightly different behaviours. This will add more variety to the game.

The appearance of new enemies could be purely random or based on how far through the game you are.

Also making the enemies worth different points if destroyed by the player would challenge the player to go after harder enemies to maximise score.

19.2.   More Complex Enemies

To also add some more excitement and challenge to the game, shooting an enemy meteor, could cause it to turn into two smaller meteors, moving in different directions.

In Astro Smash, there is a smart bomb enemy that moves rapidly towards the player and has a larger penalty, if you let it hit the planet surface.

19.3.   Extra Lives

It's nice to give the player a chance to regain lost lives. Usually added to the routine used to increase the score, it needs to consider that in our Mega Blast the player's score can also decrease, i.e., be careful that cross an extra lives marker is only rewarded once.

19.4.   Increased Difficulty

If the game stays at the same speed and does not get harder/increase its difficulty the longer the player stays alive, it will quickly become boring for the player.

For a game such as Mega Blast, the difficulty, should increase based on either how long the player has been playing or, perhaps, based on the number of enemies that have been created.

Other games might base the difficulty on the number of screens completed, or waves of enemies defeated.

19.5.   Music

In our tutorial chapter, we only added a sample of a music piece to our game, selecting or writing a more suitable piece of music will make our game come alive.

19.6.   Arcade Touches

A few more things to think of adding to give your title a professional touch would be:

- High Score Table
- Animated title screen – maybe showing the score achieved for the different enemy types
- Gameplay demo

Appendix A – ColecoVision BIOS Functions (OS 7)

This appendix contains information on the useful routines that are included in the ColecoVision's BIOS, also called OS 7. These can save you a lot of ROM space and time.

Examples are provided for some of the functions, where appropriate, either with the item or reference to an earlier section of this book if already covered.

Sound Routines

This section of routines allows you to play sound effects and music without too much effort.

Note: If you are targeting a game for the Adam Computer, you also have more functions available in Playing Sound and Music.

TURN_OFF_SOUND

Address: 1FD6h (EOS FD53h)

Stops sound on all four sound channels.

INPUT:

- None

FUNCTION(S):

- Turn off all 4 sound generators.

OUTPUTS:

- None

EXAMPLE:

```
; Turn off all sound
CALL TURN_OFF_SOUND
```

SOUND_INIT

Address: 1FEEh (EOS FD50h)

Initialises the sound and music playback buffers to use the specified RAM area.

INPUT:

- HL = LST_OF_SND_ADDRS, address in RAM to song data areas.
- B = # of song data areas to initialize.

FUNCTION(S):

- Set pointer PTR_TO_LST_OF_SND_ADDRS to LST_OF_SND_ADDRS.
- Store inactive code FF at byte 0 of the song data areas.
- Store 00 at end of song data areas.
- Sets the 4 channel sound pointers to a dummy, inactive data area.
- Initialize SAVE_CTRL to inactive code FF.
- Turn off sound

OUTPUTS:

- None

EXAMPLE:

```
; Initialise sound
LD B,SoundDataCount    ;Max number of active voices+effects
LD HL,SoundAddrs
CALL SOUND_INIT

; Example sound data setup
SoundDataCount:        EQU 4
Len_SoundDataArea:     EQU 10*SoundDataCount+1 ;7 data areas
SoundAddrs:
    DW  shoot1,SoundDataArea         ; 1  player bomb sound
    DW  shoot2,SoundDataArea+10      ; 2  player shoot sound
    DW  explode1,SoundDataArea+30    ; 3  enemy explode
    DW  0,0
```

See the chapter Sound Effects for more details on using the OS sound routines.

PLAY_IT

Address: 1FF1h (EOS FD56h)

INPUT:

- B = song number to play.

FUNCTION(S):

- If the song is already playing, do nothing.
- Otherwise,
    - Load 1st note and set NEXT_NOTE_PTR.
    - Update channel data pointers.

OUTPUTS:

- None

EXAMPLE:

```
; Play song 1 from our list of songs
LD B,1
CALL PLAY_IT
```

PLAY_SONGS

Address: 1F61h

This routine advances the current songs in progress and outputs the current frequency and attenuation data to the sound chip.

It should be called every VDP interrupt followed by **SND_MANAGER**.

INPUT:

- None

FUNCTION(S):

- Prepare and pitch the actual song notes to the sound chip.
    - Current frequency and attenuation data is output to each tone generator if sound on that
- The channel is active; otherwise, that generator is turned off.
    - Noise generator is sent current attenuation data and control data, if new.
    - Modifies SAVE_CTRL if necessary

OUTPUTS:

- None

EXAMPLE:

```
NMI:
    ; Save all registers
    PUSH  AF
    ...
    ; update our time counter
    LD HL,(TIME)
    DEC HL
    LD (TIME),HL
    ;Now we can safely call any OS7 calls
    CALL PLAY_SONGS      ; Update active music
    CALL SOUND_MAN       ; Prepare for next go at music

    ; Restore all registers
    ...
    CALL  READ_REGISTER  ; Side effect allows another NMI to happen
    POP   AF
    RETN
```

SOUND_MAN

Address: 1FF4h

Updates the current song points and counters. It should be called every VDP interrupt after PLAY_SONGS.

INPUT:

- None

FUNCTION(S):

- Update all song data areas.
    - Update counters, decrement sound duration and sweep timers.
    - Apply sound effect, modify swept frequency and attenuation values.
    - Call special effects routines where necessary.
    - Update the channel data area pointers if necessary.
    - Restart the sound if indicated.

OUTPUTS:

- None

EXAMPLE:

```
NMI:
    ; Save all registers
    PUSH AF
    …
    ; update our time counter
    LD HL,(TIME)
    DEC HL
    LD (TIME),HL
    ; Now we can safely call any OS7 calls
    CALL PLAY_SONGS    ; Update active music
    CALL SOUND_MAN     ; Prepare for next go at music

    ; Restore all registers
    …
    CALL READ_REGISTER  ; Side effect allows another NMI to happen
    POP AF
    RETN
```

Video Routines

These routines are for reading and writing to the video RAM of the TMS graphics chip.

FILL_VRAM

Address: 1F82h (EOS FD26h))

Writes DE number of times the byte value in A to VRAM starting from the address in HL.

INPUT:

- HL = Index in VRAM
- A = Byte to copy
- DE = Count

FUNCTION(S):

- Set VRAM write address to HL
- Write byte A DE times

OUTPUTS:

- None

EXAMPLE:

```
; Clear screen
LD  HL,VRAM_NAME
LD  A,0
LD  DE,768
CALL FILL_VRAM
```

GAME_OPT

Address: 1F7Ch

Displays the standard game option screen with white letters on a blue background.

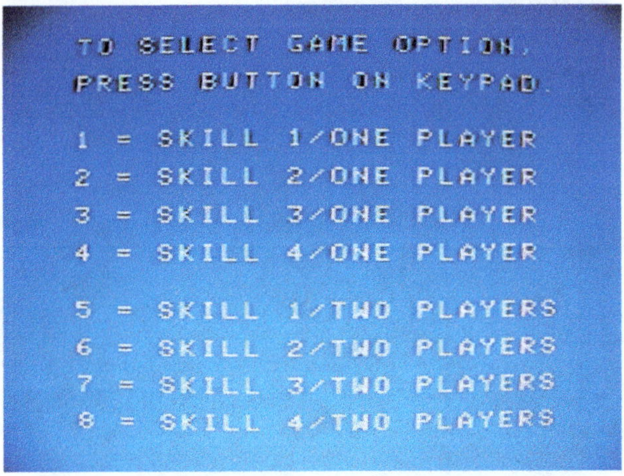

Figure 30 - ColecoVision Standard Game Option Screen

VDP is left in mode I with the VRAM memory map as follows.

Address Range	Description	Length
3800H-3FFFH	Sprite pattern table	2048 bytes
2000H-37FFH	Pattern colour table	6144 bytes
1B00H-1B7FH	Sprite attribute table	128 bytes
1800H-1AFFH	Name table	768 bytes
0000H-17FFH	Pattern table	6144 bytes

INPUT:

- None

FUNCTION(S):

- Clear VRAM
- Setup VDP Mode II
- Display the standard game option screen with white letters on a blue background.

OUTPUTS:

- None

EXAMPLE:

```
; Display the game option screen
CALL GAME_OPT
```

GET_VRAM

Address: 1FBBh (EOS FD2Fh)

Gets a certain number of bytes from a specific VRAM table and puts them in a buffer.

INPUT:

- A = TABLE_CODE
    - o   0=SPRITE_NAME_TABLE
    - o   1=SPRITE_GENERATOR_TABLE
    - o   2=PATTERN_NAME_TABLE
    - o   3=PATTERN_GENERATOR_TABLE
    - o   4=COLOR_TABLE
- DE = START_INDEX
- HL = DATA_BUFFER
- IY = COUNT

FUNCTION(S):

- Reads the bytes from video RAM and copies them into the supplied memory location.

OUTPUTS:

- None

EXAMPLE:

```
; Get the top part of the name table
LD  A,2      ; Pattern Name Table
LD  DE,0     ; Top of the table
LD  HL,BUFFER ; our local buffer
LD  IY,256   ; number of bytes to get (and the size of our buffer)
CALL GET_VRAM
```

INIT_SPR_ORDER

Address: 1FC1h

Initialises the Sprite Order list to the default order - 0 to 31.

The Sprite Order list is used by the WR_SPR_NM_TBL function to determine what order the sprites are written to video RAM.

INPUT:

- A = Sprite count – The length of the sprite order table, which would be the same as the intended number of entries in the local sprite attribute table

FUNCTION(S):

- Sets the Sprite Order list to the default order - 0 to 31

OUTPUTS:

- None

EXAMPLE:

```
; Set default sprite order
LD A, SPRITE_COUNT
CALL INIT_SPR_ORDER
```

INIT_TABLE

Address: 1FB8h (EOS FD29h)

Initialises the table addresses for the VRAM tables and writes the appropriate base addresses to the VDP register.

INPUT:

- A = TABLE_CODE
    - 0=SPRITE_NAME_TABLE
    - 1=SPRITE_GENERATOR_TABLE
    - 2=PATTERN_NAME_TABLE
    - 3=PATTERN_GENERATOR_TABLE
    - 4=COLOR_TABLE
- HL = Address in VRAM to set the table to

FUNCTION(S):

- Save the table address for the specified table in the VRAM_ADDR_TABLE
- Update the VDP Status registers
- Initialise the table in VRAM with default values

OUTPUTS:

- The addresses used for the VDP tables are stored in the VRAM_ADDR_TABLE (73F2-73FB).

EXAMPLE:

```
; Set the pattern name table address
LD A,2
LD HL,$1800
CALL INIT_TABLE
```

LOAD_ASCII

Address: 1F7Fh (EOS FD38h)

Writes out ASCII character generators to the pattern generator table.

INIT_TABLE must be used to set up the table address.

INPUT:

- None

FUNCTION(S):

- Copies the ASCII character patterns stored in OS ROM to the VRAM pattern generator table.

OUTPUTS:

- None

EXAMPLE:

```
; load the ASCII character patterns into VRAM
CALL LOAD_ASCII
```

MODE_1

Address: 1F85h

Sets up the VDP to be in screen mode 1 (TMS Graphics Mode II). Uses INIT_TABLE to set the VDP addresses.

INPUT:

- None

FUNCTION(S):

- Set VDP to be in Graphics Mode II with the following VDP addresses for the pattern, colour, name and sprite details

Address Range	Area	Length
0000h-17FFh	Pattern table	6144 bytes
2000h-37FFh	Colour table	6144 bytes
1800h-1AFFh	Name table	768 bytes
1B00h-1B7Fh	Sprite Attribute table	128 bytes
3800h-3FFFh	Sprite Pattern table	2048 bytes

-

OUTPUTS:

- None

EXAMPLE:

```
; Set VDP Mode 1
CALL   MODE_1
```

PUT_VRAM

Address: 1FBEh (EOS FD2Ch)

Writes a certain number of bytes to VRAM from a buffer.

INPUT:

- A = TABLE_CODE
    - o 0=SPRITE_NAME_TABLE
    - o 1=SPRITE_GENERATOR_TABLE
    - o 2=PATTERN_NAME_TABLE
    - o 3=PATTERN_GENERATOR_TABLE
    - o 4=COLOR_TABLE
- DE = START_INDEX
- HL = DATA_BUFFER
- IY = COUNT

FUNCTION(S):

- Set the VDP write address based on the table and starting offset
- Copy each byte from RAM and write to VRAM

OUTPUTS:

- None

EXAMPLE:

```
; Write title screen data to middle section of the screen
LD A,2
LD DE,256
LD HL,TITLESCREEN
LD IY,256
CALL PUT_VRAM
```

READ_REGISTER

Address: 1FDCh (EOS FD23h)

Get the value of the VDP status register.

Note: After reading the VDP status register the VDP is clear to send the next vBlank when it occurs, which could be immediately.

INPUT:

- None

FUNCTION(S):

- Get the VDP status register

OUTPUTS:

- A contains the current value of the VDP status register

EXAMPLE:

```
; end of NMI routine, signal clear to generate next vBlank
CALL READ_REGISTER
POP AF
RETN
```

READ_VRAM

Address: 1FE2h (EOS FD1Dh)

Read one or more values from VRAM into a RAM buffer.

INPUT:

- HL = Address of the first byte of the RAM buffer to write to
- DE = Address in VRAM to start reading from
- BC = Number of bytes to read from VRAM

FUNCTION(S):

- Set VRAM read address to DE
- Read VRAM byte and write to address in HL
- Increment HL and decrement BC
- Repeat until BC zero

OUTPUTS:

None

EXAMPLE:

```
; Get first 256 bytes of pattern name table
LD HL, BUFFER
LD DE, VRAM_NAME
LD BC, 256
CALL READ_VRAM
```

WRITE_REGISTER

Address: 1FD9h (EOS FD20h)

Write a new value to one of the VDP registers.

INPUT:

- B = register to write to
- C = value to write the register

FUNCTION(S):

- Output the value to the specified register and update the RAM copy of the register.

OUTPUTS:

- None

EXAMPLE:

```
SETSCREEN2:
    LD BC,0002h        ;Reg 0: Mode 2
    CALL WRITE_REGISTER
    LD BC,0206h        ; Name table 1800h
    CALL WRITE_REGISTER
    LD BC,03ffh        ; Colour table 2000h
    CALL WRITE_REGISTER
```

WRITE_VRAM

Address: 1FDFh (EOS FD1Ah)

Write one or more values to VRAM

INPUT:

- HL = Address of the first byte to transfer
- DE = Address in VRAM to write to
- BC = Number of bytes to write to VRAM

FUNCTION(S):

- Set VRAM write address to DE
- Write byte in HL to VRAM
- Increment HL and decrement BC
- Repeat until BC zero

OUTPUTS:

- None

EXAMPLE:

```
; Write top of pattern name table from buffer
LD HL,BUFFER
LD DE,VRAM_NAME
LD BC,256
CALL WRITE_VRAM
```

WR_SPR_NM_TBL (EOS WR_SPR_ATTRIBUT)

Address: 1FC4h (EOS FD1Ah)

Writes **SPRITE_NAME_TABLE** to VRAM in the order defined in the sprite order list.

INPUT:

- A = Number of sprites to write

FUNCTION(S):

- Iterates through the list of sprites defined in the order list and writes them to VRAM.

OUTPUTS:

- None

EXAMPLE:

```
; Write sprite name table to VRAM
LD A,32 ; write all sprites
CALL WR_SPR_NM_TBL
```

Object Routines

These routines are for controlling complex objects made up of both character tiles and/or sprites.

These routines are very complex, use quite a bit of RAM (and BIOS ROM space) and are often not the fastest way of doing object manipulation.

They were most likely not used much past the initial set of games released for the ColecoVision by the original in-house development team.

They also have a couple of bugs, making them not a good choice unless you patch them in your own title's ROM area.

ACTIVATE

Address: 1FF7

ACTIVATE is used to initialize the RAM status area for the object and move its pattern and colour definitions to the PATTERN and COLOR tables in VRAM.

The second function is enabled or disabled by setting or resetting the carry flag in the PSW. This is necessary to prevent sending the same graphics data to VRAM more than once when creating identical objects.

The calling sequence for activating an object is as follows:

```
LD HL,OBJ_n ; ->OBJ to activate
SCF          ; Signal Move to VRAM
CALL ACTIVATE
```

OR

```
LD HL,OBJ_n ; ->OBJ to activate
OR A         ; Don't Move to VRAM
CALL ACTIVATE
```

VDP_MODE_WORD (73C3), WORK_BUFFER (8006) may be needed by called subroutines. AF , HL, DE, BC and IY are affected. Additional registers may be changed by called subroutines.

OBJECT HEADER:

Pointer to OBJ GEN CPU ROM, pointer to OBJ CPU RAM.

The OBJ GEN CPU ROM header starts with a less significant nibble (LSN) as OBJ TYPE.

OBJ TYPE:

- 0 = semi-mobile,
- 1 = mobile,
- 2 = 0sprite,
- 3 = 1sprite,
- Other = complex.

BUG Error in subroutine for semi-mobile type objects in graphic mode I.

INPUT:

- HL = pointer to the object data. Carry flag = is set to move graphic data to VRAM, reset otherwise.

FUNCTION(S):

- Initialize the RAM status area for the object point to by HL
- If the carry flag is set, move object pattern and colour generators to the PATTERN and COLOR generator tables in VRAM.

OUTPUTS:

- None

CALC_OFFSET

Address: 08c0h (EOS FD32h)

INPUT:

- D = Y_PAT_POS.
- E = X_PAT_POS.

FUNCTION(S):

- This routine calculates the proper offset into the name table for the pattern position given by X_PAT_POS, Y_PAT_POS.
- The formula used is:
  - offset = 32* Y_PAT_POS + X_PAT_POS

OUTPUTS:

- DE = offset.

EXAMPLE:

```
;This routine writes a message to a particular location on the screen.
LD E,10            ; goto line 10.
LD D,5             ; column 5.
CALL CALC_OFFSET ; get offset.
LD A,2             ; name table.
EX DE,HL           ; put first entry into DE.
LD HL,MESSAGE      ; print this word.
LD IY,11           ; it is 11 bytes long.
CALL PUT_VRAM      ; put in in VRAM.
.....
MESSAGE:
 DB 'Please Wait'
```

GET_BKGRND

Address: 0898h

Gets a box of names (characters) from screen.

INPUT:

- HL = location in CPU RAM to copy names from VRAM
- E = X_PAT_POS
- D = Y_PAT_POS
- C = X_EXTENT
- B = Y_EXTENT

FUNCTION(S):

- Gets the names from the name table which constitute the background in which an object is to be moved at X_PAT_POS, Y_PAT_POS.

OUTPUTS:

- None.

EXAMPLE:

```
; get a 10 x 10 box of characters values from the screen
; Note: RAMBUFFER needs to be 100 bytes long!
LD HL, RAMBUFFER
LD E, 10 ; top left X position
LD D, 10 ; top left Y position
LD C, 10 ; width of box
LD B, 10 ; height of box
CALL GET_BKGRND
```

INIT_WRITER

Address: 1FE5h

Initialises the queue used for deferred writing to VRAM.

INPUT:

- A = size of the deferred write queue.
- HL = location in RAM of the deferred write queue.

FUNCTION(S):

- Initialize deferred write queue in RAM:
    - QUEUE_SIZE (73CA) = A
    - QUEUE_HEAD (73CB) = 0
    - QUEUE_TAIL (73CC) = 0
    - HEAD_ADDRESS (73CD-73CE) = HL
    - TAIL_ADDRESS (73CF-73D0) = HL

OUTPUTS:

- None

EXAMPLE:

```
; Initialise the deferred write queue
LD A,10 ; allow ten items
LD HL,WRITE_QUEUE
```

PUTCOMPLEX

Address: 0EA2h

The position and frame number of each of a complex object's component objects is updated.

Then PUT_OBJECT is called for each of the component objects.

METHOD OF COMBINING OBJECT PATTERNS

1. Object pattern OR'ed with background pattern color1 of background changed to mobile object's colour if corresponding pattern byte not zero
2. Replace background pattern with object pattern treat colour same as #1
3. Same as #1 except color0 changed to transparent
4. Same as #2 except color0 changed to transparent

INPUT:

- IX = Address of object to be processed
- HL = Address of object's graphics tables in ROM
- B = Selector for method of combining object generators with background generators
- C = Object type, and number of components

OUTPUTS:

- None

PUT_FRAME

Address: 080Bh

Puts a box of names (characters) on screen. It prevents bleeding outside visible screen.

INPUT:

- HL = address of list of names (characters that compose the frame)
- E = X_PAT_POS
- D = Y_PAT_POS
- C = X_EXTENT
- B = Y_EXTENT

FUNCTION(S):

- The names which constitute a frame are moved to the name table in VRAM.
- The upper left-hand corner of the frame is positioned at X_PAT_POS, Y_PAT_POS.

OUTPUTS:

- None.

EXAMPLE:

```
; put a frame of characters on the screen
LD HL, NAME_TBL
LD E, 10 ; X = 10
LD D, 10 ; Y = 10
LD C, 10 ; 10 characters wide
LD B, 10 ; 10 characters high
CALL PUT_FRAME
```

PUT_MOBILE

Address: 0A87h

This procedure places a mobile object on the pattern plane at the X, Y pixel localisation specified in that object's RAM status AREA.

The size of a mobile object Is fixed in two-by-two pattern blocks. They belong to the pattern plane but can be moved from pixel to pixel in X, Y directions like a sprite superimposed on the background. However, the speed of mobile objects are too slow when compared to the sprites.

METHOD OF COMBINING OBJECT GENERATORS

1. Object pattern gens OR'ed with background pattern gens color1 of background changed to mobile object's colour if corresponding pattern byte not zero
2. Replace background pattern gens with object pattern gens. treat colour same as #1
3. Same as #1 except color0 changed to transparent
4. Same as #2 except color0 changed to transparent

Object Pattern Data Definition

The following are offsets from the start of the free buffer area.

These locations used to store variables and pattern and colour data.

Label	Offset	Description
YDISP	0	Y Displacement
XDISP	1	X Displacement
COLR	2	Colour
FLAGS	3	BITS 0,1=Selector#, BIT X = Graphics Mode (I/II)
FRM	4	Frame to be Displayed
F_GEN	5	Name of 1st generator in object's gen table
YP_OS	7	Y_PAT_POS of OLD_SCREEN
XP_OS	6	X_PAT_POS of OLD_SCREEN
YP_BK	18	Y_PAT_POS of BACKGROUND ;12h
XP_BK	17	X_PAT_POS of BACKGROUND ;11h
BK_PTN	28	Start of background pattern generators ; 1Ch
OBJ_PTN	100	Start of object's pattern generators ; 64h
BK_CLR	132	Start of background colour generators ; 84h

INPUT:

- IX = Address of object to be processed
- HL = Address of object's graphics tables in ROM
- B = Selector for method of combining object generators with background generators

OUTPUTS:

- None

PUTOBJ

Address: 1FFA

Vectors to one of 5 specific routines for placing the different object types on the display.

In addition, this module contains routines that allow operations to be deferred, typically until an interrupt occurs, and performed in a block by central WRITER routine.

According to flag DEFER_WRITES (73C6), this function updates the object specifications (position x/y, pattern, colour) of object IX on screen or puts the object in the queue for updating later.

INPUT:

- IX = Object data pointer
- B = Object parameter, selector for methods of combining object generators with background generators (for mobile objects only)

FUNCTION(S):

- Check if DEFER_WRITES flag (73C6) is true.
- If true, set up for deferred write by calling SET_UP_WRITE
- If not, process object by calling DO_PUTOBJ

OUTPUTS:

- None

EXAMPLE:

```
LD IX, OBJ_DEP
LD B, BKGND_SELECT
CALL PUTOBJ
```

PUTSEMI

Address:

Puts semi-mobile objects on screen.

A semi-mobile object is a rectangular block of tiles that can be positioned anywhere on screen.

INPUT:

- IX = Address of object to be processed
- HL = Address of object's graphics tables in ROM

FUNCTION(S):

- It calls PX_TO_PTRN_POS and CALC_OFFSET to calculate the top-left current screen XY position of the box of chars in RAM.
- Checks if chars that will be overwritten must be saved (OLD_SCREEN in Semi Object Table.)
- If Yes (< 8000h):
  - It recalls the names (characters) that were overwritten the last time (if present) from RAM (OLD_SCREEN) and put them back on screen.
  - It calls GET_BKGRND to save the names (characters) that the new box will overwrite in RAM (again, 3rd word in Semi Object Table.)
  - It finally writes new box of names (characters) on screen by calling PUT_VRAM.

Notes:

- OLD_SCREEN can be in RAM (7100h to 7FFFh) or in VRAM (0000h-3FFFh).
- Be sure to use the ranges of addresses specified here (possibility of problems).
- If using VRAM for OLD_SCREEN, it uses the WORK_BUFFER (8006) pointer for temporary storage.
- Else (>= 8000) Only write new box of names (characters) on screen by calling PUT_VRAM

OUTPUTS:

- None

PUTOSPRITE

Address: 08DFh

Defines a set of sprite patterns and places one or more sprites on the screen.

The format for sprite objects is (Pascal Syntax):

```
SPRITE_OBJECT = RECORD
GRAPHICS:^SPRITE_GRAPHICS
STATUS:^SPRITE_STATUS
SPRITE_INDEX:BYTE (SPRITE_NAME_TABLE index of this sprite)
END SPRITE_OBJECT

SPRITE_GRAPHICS = RECORD
OBJECT_TYPE:BYTE
FIRST_GEN_NAME:BYTE (Name of the 1st sprite generators)
PTRN_POINTER:^PATTERN_GENERATOR (Pointer to ROM'ed generators)
NUMGEN:BYTE (Number of ROM'ed generators)
FRAME_TABLE_PTR:^ARRAY[0..nn] of FRAME (table of animation frames)
END SPRITE_ROM_GRAPHICS

SPRITE_STATUS = RECORD
FRAME:BYTE (Current animation frame)
X_LOCATION:INTEGER
Y_LOCATION:INTEGER
NEXT_GEN:BYTE (Index of free space in generator table)
END SPRITE_STATUS

FRAME = RECORD
COLOR:BYTE (Sprite's colour for this frame)
SHAPE:BYTE (This frame's offset from name from FIRST_GEN_NAME)
END FRAME

SPRITE = RECORD
Y:BYTE
X:BYTE
NAME:BYTE
COLOR_AND_TAG:BYTE
END SPRITE
```

INPUT:

- IX = Address of the sprite object

OUTPUTS:

- None

PX_TO_PTRN_POS

Address: 07E8h (EOS FD35h)

Used to determine the tile pattern number for a given offset.

INPUT:

- DE = signed 16-bit number.

FUNCTION(S):

- Divides DE by 8
- If signed result > 127 then E = max signed positive number 127.
- If signed result < -128 then E = min negative number -128.

OUTPUTS:

- E = DE/8, except if DE/8 < -128 or DE/8 > 127 then E equals respectively -128 or 127.

SET_UP_WRITE

Address: 0623h

Sets up a deferred VRAM write operation.

INPUT:

- IX = data pointer.
- B = Object parameter, selector for methods of combining object generators with background generators (for mobile objects only)

FUNCTION(S):

- Put data pointer address at the head of the deferred write queue, followed by the B parameter value.
- The write data is the same as if calling PUTOBJ

OUTPUTS:

- None

EXAMPLE:

```
; add a deferred write operation to the queue
LD IX, WRITE_DATA
LD B, 1
CALL SET_UP_WRITE
```

WRITER

Address: 1FE8h (EOS FD3Bh)

Writes any queued deferred writes to VRAM.

Call during VDP interrupt if deferred writing is used.

INPUT:

- None.

FUNCTION(S):

- Temporary reset deferred write flag and write data at queue to VRAM.

OUTPUTS:

- None

EXAMPLE:

```
; Write any deferred writes to VRAM
CALL WRITER
```

Timer Routines

The user must reserve two free RAM spaces to use timers.

The first RAM space is for the timer table itself. The second one is for the extra data block needed for repeating long-timers.

The following data structures are what the timers look like in RAM.

Note:

To tell whether a ColecoVision runs at 50Hz or 60Hz, the ROM address $0069 (AMERICA), contains how many ticks per second i.e. 50 or 60 respectively.

Timer Data Structures

General timer data structure (3 bytes):

TIMER	DONE	REPEAT	FREE	EOT	LONG	-	-	-
?								
?								

Specific timer data structures:

ONE-TIME SHORT TIMER

DONE	0	0	0	0	-	-	-
Unsigned counter value							
-							

REPEATING SHORT TIMER

DONE	1	0	0	0	-	-	-
Unsigned current counter value							
Unsigned original counter value							

ONE-TIME LONG TIMER

DONE	0	0	0	1	-	-	-
Unsigned counter value - low-part LSB							
Unsigned counter value - high-part MSB							

REPEATING LONG TIMER

DONE	1	0	0	1	-	-	
Pointer to a data block							
for extra timer information							

DATA BLOCK

Unsigned current counter value - low-part LSB
Unsigned current counter value - high-part MSB
Unsigned original counter value - low-part LSB
Unsigned original counter value - high-part MSB

FREE_SIGNAL

Address: 1FCAh

Stop the specified timer and release the memory block it was allocated.

INPUT:

- A = signal (timer) number to be freed.
  - 0 = 1st signal, 1 = 2nd signal, etc.

FUNCTION(S):

- Finds signal (timer) A, stops it by setting bit 5 (FREE) and release its data block if exists.

OUTPUTS:

- None.

EXAMPLE:

```
; free our signal timer
LD A,(TickTimer)
CALL FREE_SIGNAL
```

INIT_TIMER

Address: 1FC7h

Initialise the supplied timer memory structures.

INPUT:

- HL = base address in CPU RAM for timer table.
- DE = base address in CPU RAM for data block.

FUNCTION(S):

- Store given base address for timer table in **TIMER_TABLE_BASE** (73D3-73D4) and for data block in **NEXT_TIMER_DATA_BYTE** (73D5-73D6).

OUTPUTS:

- None.

EXAMPLE:

```
; initialise clock
LD HL,TIMER_TABLE
LD DE,TIMER_DATA_BLOCK
CALL INIT_TIMER
```

REQUEST_SIGNAL

Address: 1FCDh

Setup a timer of length HL. The timer can be singular or repeat indefinitely.

INPUT:

- HL = length of timer
- A = repeating timer if 0, non-repeating type if not.

FUNCTION(S):

- Search for a free signal (timer) and initialize it with HL and A.
- Return signal (timer) number used in A.

OUTPUTS:

- A = signal (timer) number.

EXAMPLE:

```
; Create and enable standard timers
CREATE_TIMERS:
    LD HL,(AMERICA)       ; How long a second is
    SRA L
    LD H,0
    LD A,1                ; set to repeating
    CALL REQUEST_SIGNAL
    LD (HalfSecTimer),A   ; Happens once per half second
    LD HL,(AMERICA)       ; How long a second is
    SRA L
    SRA L
    LD H,0
    LD A,1                ; set to repeating
    CALL REQUEST_SIGNAL
    LD (QtrSecTimer),A    ; Happens once per quarter second
    LD HL,1
    LD A,1                ; set to repeating
    CALL REQUEST_SIGNAL
    LD (TickTimer),A      ; Happens once per tick
    RET
```

TEST_SIGNAL

Address: 1FD0h

Checks whether the specified signal has occurred.

INPUT:

- A = signal (timer) number to be tested.

FUNCTION(S):

- Check if the signal (timer) number exists.
- If so, return A = true if bit 7 (DONE) is set
- If a non-repeating timer, then free the signal (timer). Otherwise, return A = false

OUTPUTS:

- A = true if signal bit 7 (DONE) is set, false otherwise.

EXAMPLE:

```
MLOOP:
    ; check that a base tick has occurred
    ; ensures consistent movement speed between 50 & 60Hz systems
    LD A,(TickTimer)
    CALL TEST_SIGNAL
    OR A
    JR Z,MLOOP
```

TIME_MGR

Address: 1FD3h

Update all timers in the timer table, called once per VDP interrupt.

INPUT:

- None.

FUNCTION(S):

- Get timer table address from **TIMER_TABLE_BASE** (73D3-73D4). Update all timers in timer table.

OUTPUTS:

- None.

EXAMPLE:

```
NMI:
        PUSH  AF
        PUSH  BC
        PUSH  DE
        PUSH  HL
        PUSH  IX
        PUSH  IY
        EX    AF,AF'
        PUSH  AF
        EXX
        PUSH  BC
        PUSH  DE
        PUSH  HL
        ; update our time counter
        LD HL,(TIME)
        DEC HL
        LD (TIME),HL
        ; Now we can safely call any OS7 calls
        CALL PLAY_SONGS   ; Update active music
        CALL SOUND_MAN    ; Prepare for next go at music
        ; write sprite table
        CALL SPRWRT
        LD A,(VDU_HOOK)
        CP 0cdh
        JR NZ,NMI2
        CALL VDU_HOOK
NMI2:
        CALL TIME_MGR
```

Controller Routines

This section of routines provides functions that decode input from the various ColecoVision controllers.

Each normal controller has a joystick, left and right fire buttons, and a number pad containing ten digits along with the * and # buttons.

The Super Controllers add two more fire buttons and a spinner controller.

The Roller Controller uses the two spinner controller ports for X & Y movement.

Note:

- The extra push buttons (Fire 3 and Fire 4) for the Super Action Controllers were done after the ColecoVision Bios, so they are not decoded by calling **DECODER** or **POLLER**.
- The information from a controller is read by the CPU on eight input lines through a single port (see **CONT_SCAN**).
- Once a port has been read, the input data must be decoded.

	D_6	D_5	INT	D_3	D_2	D_1	D_0	
Fire	X							Common 0
North				X				Enabled
N-E				X	X			By ports
East					X			FD, FF
S-E					X	X		
South					X			
S-W					X	X		
West							X	
N-W				X			X	
Arm (Fire 2)	X							Common 1
2				X				Enabled
3						X	X	By ports
6							X	FC, FE
9					X			
8				X	X	X		
7				X	X			
4				X	X		X	
1					X			
5				X	X			
0					X		X	
*				X	X			
#				X			X	
Fire 3					X	X	X	
Fire 4				X		X	X	
Spinner A			X					Always
Spinner B (presently used in Expansion Mod #2)		X						Function

Keypad:

1	2	3
4	5	6
7	8	9
*	0	#

Note:

- D4 is named INT in the ColecoVision official documentation, including the absolute OS 7' bios listing.
- When a spinner is spinning, INT bit (Spinner A) is reset and D5 bit (Spinner B) is set or reset depending on the way the spinner is spinning

ARM_DBNCE

Address: 12E9h

ARM button debounce routine.

INPUT:

- A = Raw data
- IX = Controller memory pointer
- IY = Debounce status buffer

OUTPUT:

- (IY + 7) = debounced data

EXAMPLE:

```
; read raw data from controller 0
LD H,0
CALL CONT_READ
; A contains raw controller data
LD IX, S0_C0
LD IY, DBNCE_BUFF
CALL ARM_DBNCE
```

CONT_READ

Address: 113Dh

Because the returned value in register A is the complement of the controller port data, bits equalling 1 mean data, and bits equalling 0 mean no data. Only register A is affected.

INPUT:

- H = 0 for player #1, 1 for player #2.

FUNCTION(S):

- Return the complement value of the controller port H segment 0 data (joystick data).

OUTPUTS:

- A = Raw data from controller H

EXAMPLE:

```
; read raw data from controller 0
LD H,0
CALL CONT_READ
```

CONTROLLER_INIT

Address: 1105h

Initialise controller

CONTROLLER_MAP (8008), **DBNCE_BUFF** (73D7-73D8) are needed. A, B, IX, IY are affected.

INPUT:

- None (although value of A is used?)

FUNCTION(S):

- Initialize controller to strobe reset.
- Clear controller memory and debounce status buffer.
- Clear remaining variables:
    - SPIN_SW0_CT (73EB): Spinner counter port #1
    - SPIN_SW1_CT (73EC): Spinner counter port #2
    - S0_C0 (73EE): Segment #0 data, port #1
    - S0_C1 (73EF): Segment #0 data, port #2
    - S1_C0 (73F0): Segment #1 data, port #1
    - S1_C1 (73F1): Segment #1 data, port #2

OUTPUTS:

- None

EXAMPLE:

```
; Initialise controller
XOR A
CALL CONTROLLER_INIT
```

CONTROLLER_SCAN

Address: 1F76h

Controller scanner routine.

Because the returned value in register A is the complement of the controller port data, bits equalling 1 mean data, and bits equalling 0 mean no data.

INPUT:

- None

FUNCTION(S):

- Update SO_CO, S0_C1, S1_C0, S1_C1 by reading segments 0 and 1 from both controller ports.

OUTPUT:

- None

EXAMPLE:

```
; Scan controllers for changes
CALL CONTROLLER_SCAN
```

DECODER

Address: 1F79h

This routine returns the decoded raw, un-debounced data from a joystick controller.

INPUT:

- H = Controller number (0 for player #1, 1 for player #2)
- L = Segment number (0 for fire + joystick, 1 for arm + keyboard)

FUNCTION(S):

- If L = segment number 0 - Load spinner counter SPIN_SW0_CT or SPIN_SW1_CT in E
  - Call CONT_SCAN
  - Load joystick data in L (A AND 0F)
  - Load Fire state in H (A AND 40)
- Else
  - L = segment number 1
  - Call CONT_SCAN
  - Load decoded key value in L (0 = key 0, ... , 9 = key 9, A = key *, B = key #, F = no key)
  - Load Arm state in H (A AND 40)

OUTPUT:

- H = State of Fire (if segment number = 0), Arm (if segment number = 1)
- L = State of Joystick (if segment number = 0), Keyboard (if segment number = 1)
- E = Spinner (if segment number = 0)

EXAMPLE:

```
LD H,0 ; controller 0
LD L,0 ; controller segment number
CALL DECODER
```

FIRE_DBNCE

Address: 1289h

Fire debounce routine.

INPUT:

- A = Raw data
- IX = Controller memory pointer
- IY = Debounce status buffer

OUTPUT:

- (IY + 1) = debounced data

EXAMPLE:

```
; read raw data from controller 0
LD H,0
CALL CONT_READ
; A contains raw controller data
LD IX, S0_C0
LD IY, DBNCE_BUFF
CALL FIRE_DBNCE
```

JOY_DBNCE

Address: 12B9h

Joystick debounce routine.

INPUT:

- A = Raw data
- IX = Controller memory pointer
- IY = Debounce status buffer

OUTPUT:

- (IY + 3) = debounced data

EXAMPLE:

```
; read raw data from controller 0
LD H,0
CALL CONT_READ
; A contains raw controller data
LD IX, S0_C0
LD IY, DBNCE_BUFF
CALL JOY_DBNCE
```

KBD_DBNCE

Address: 1250h

Keyboard debounce routine.

INPUT:

- A = Raw data
- IX = Controller memory pointer
- IY = Debounce status buffer

OUTPUT:

- (IY + 9) = debounced data

EXAMPLE:

```
; read raw data from controller 0
LD H,0
CALL CONT_READ
; A contains raw controller data
LD IX, S0_C0
LD IY, DBNCE_BUFF
CALL KBD_DBNCE
```

POLLER

Address: 1FEBh (EOS FD3Eh)

Polling routine for all devices in controller.

INPUT:

- A = Controller/spinner
  Bit 0 = Controller 0,
  Bit 1 = Controller 1,
  Bit 7 = Enable spinner for selected Controller
- IX = Where to place the decoded data (10 bytes required)

FUNCTION(S):

- Check status of player 0, if active
  - Store status using Decode methods for segments 0 and 1
- Check status of player 1, if active
  - Store status using Decode methods for segments 0 and 1

OUTPUT:

- None

EXAMPLE:

```
; get state of both controllers
LD A,3
LD IX,TABLE    ; put data here
CALL POLLER
LD IX,TABLE    ; restore pointer
LD A,(IX+1)    ; get the right button
OR (IX+2)      ; or with the left button
JR NZ,PUSHED   ; at least one button pushed
```

UPDATE_SPINNER

Address: 1F88h (EOS FD41h)

This routine checks the spinner value in both joysticks, incrementing or decrementing the internal spin table if either is active.

To be able to detect the number of data updates generated by the spinners, especially from the roller controller, it is best calling this routine in your NMI routine.

And then using the current values stored in **SPIN_SW0_CT** and **SPIN_SW1_CT**.

INPUT:

None

FUNCTION(S):

- Update counters pointed by **SPIN_SW0_CT** and **SPIN_SW1_CT** by reading bits 4 and 5 from segment 1 of both controller ports.

OUTPUT:

- None

EXAMPLE:

```
; get the current spinner values from both controller ports
CALL UPDATE_SPINNER
```

Graphics Primitives

This is a package of routines that allow application programmers to operate on graphic tile patterns.

Each of them takes, as inputs, an area in one of the pattern tables in which the patterns to be operated upon reside, a count of the patterns to use, and an area of the same table into which the results are to be put.

The only RAM area they use is the **WORK_BUFFER**, a pointer, which points to a location in user RAM, defined by the programmer.

Table Codes:

- 0=SPRITE_NAME_TABLE
- 1=SPRITE_PATTERN_TABLE
- 2=TILE_NAME_TABLE
- 3=TILE_PATTERN_TABLE
- 4=COLOR_TABLE

NOTE:

These routines are written and read without the possibility of deferral and should not be used in any situation where they may be interrupted.

ENLARGE

Address: 1F73h

It takes each of block of COUNT character or sprite patterns following SOURCE in the specified TABLE_CODE and enlarges it into a block of four patterns where each pixel of the original pattern is expanded to four pixels in the new ones.

If the patterns are from the pattern plane and the graphics mode is 2, then it also quadruples each of the corresponding colour patterns as well.

INPUTS:

- A = TABLE_CODE
- DE = SOURCE – Two-byte index of the first entry in the specified table
- HL = DESTINATION – Two-byte index of the first entry in the specified table
- BC = COUNT – Two-byte count of the number of entries to be processed

FUNCTION(S):

- It takes each of block of character or sprite patterns and enlarges it into a block of four patterns where each pixel of the original pattern is expanded to four pixels in the new ones.
- If the patterns are from the pattern plane and the graphics mode is 2, then it also quadruples each of the corresponding colour patterns as well.

OUTPUTS:

- None

EXAMPLE:

```
; enlarge the 1st character pattern to four characters patterns
LD A, 2 ; tile pattern table
LD DE, 0 ; first tile pattern
LD HL, 1 ; second tile pattern
LD BC, 1 ; only process one pattern
CALL ENLARGE
```

REFLECT_HORZONTAL

Address: 1F6Dh

Takes each pattern in a block of COUNT patterns following the SOURCE in the table indicated by TABLE_CODE and modifies in such a way that the new pattern this created will appear to be a reflection about the horizontal screen axis of the old.

The created patterns are put back into a block of COUNT patterns following the DESTINATION address in the same table.

If the patterns are from the pattern plane and the graphics mode is 2, then the routine also copies the corresponding colour patterns. Otherwise, it assumes that the colour data has already been set up.

INPUTS:

- A = TABLE_CODE
- DE = SOURCE – Two-byte index of the first entry in the specified table
- HL = DESTINATION – Two-byte index of the first entry in the specified table
- BC = COUNT – Two-byte count of the number of entries to be processed

OUTPUTS:

- None

EXAMPLE:

```
; Reflect horizontally the 1st sprite pattern, into the 2nd sprite pattern
LD A, 1 ; sprite table
LD DE, 0 ; first sprite pattern
LD HL, 1 ; second sprite pattern
LD BC, 1 ; only process one pattern
CALL REFLECT_HORIZONTAL
```

REFLECT_VERTICAL

Address: 1F6Ah

Takes each pattern in a block of COUNT patterns following the SOURCE in the table indicated by TABLE_CODE and modifies in such a way that the new pattern this created will appear to be a reflection about the vertical screen axis of the old.

The created patterns are put back into a block of COUNT patterns following the DESTINATION address in the same table.

If the patterns are from the pattern plane and the graphics mode is 2, then the routine also copies the corresponding colour patterns. Otherwise, it assumes that the colour data has already been set up.

INPUTS:

- A = TABLE_CODE
- DE = SOURCE – Two-byte index of the first entry in the specified table
- HL = DESTINATION – Two-byte index of the first entry in the specified table
- BC = COUNT – Two-byte count of the number of entries to be processed

OUTPUTS:

- None

EXAMPLE:

```
; Reflect vertically the 1st sprite pattern, into the 2nd sprite pattern
LD A, 1 ; sprite table
LD DE, 0 ; first sprite pattern
LD HL, 1 ; second sprite pattern
LD BC, 1 ; only process one pattern
CALL REFLECT_VERTICAL
```

ROTATE_90

Address: 1F70h

Takes each pattern in a block of COUNT patterns starting from SOURCE in the table indicated by TABLE_CODE and modifies it in such a way that the new pattern will be a 90-degree clockwise rotation of the old pattern.

The created pattern will be put back into a block of COUNT patterns starting from DESTINATION in the same table.

If the generators are from the pattern plane and the graphics mode is 2, then it copies the corresponding colour entries as well.

Care must be taken if rotating tile patterns in mode 2 as the corresponding colour patterns have to conform to the two colours per row limit.

INPUTS:

- A = TABLE_CODE
- DE = SOURCE – Two-byte index of the first entry in the specified table
- HL = DESTINATION – Two-byte index of the first entry in the specified table
- BC = COUNT – Two-byte count of the number of entries to be processed

OUTPUTS:

- None

EXAMPLE:

```
; Rotate the 1st sprite pattern, into the 2nd sprite pattern
LD A, 1 ; sprite table
LD DE, 0 ; first sprite pattern
LD HL, 1 ; second sprite pattern
LD BC, 1 ; only process one pattern
CALL ROTATE_90
```

Miscellaneous Functions

This section contains several general-purpose utility functions plus the routines called as part of the consoles boot up process.

ADD816

Address: 01B1 (EOS FD4Dh)

Adds 8-bit two's complement signed value passed in A to the 16-bit value pointed to by HL.

INPUT:

- HL = pointer to a word value.
- A = signed byte value [-128,127].

FUNCTION(S):

- Adds 8-bit two's complement signed value passed in A to the 16-bit value pointed to by HL.

OUTPUTS:

- (HL) = (HL) + A

EXAMPLE:

```
; update score
LD  HL,SCORE
LD  A,10
CALL ADD816
```

BOOT_UP

Address: 0000h

Primary console start-up procedure.

INPUT:

- None

FUNCTION(S):

- Set stack (= 073B9h) Continue the execution by calling POWER_UP

OUTPUTS:

- None

EXAMPLE:

```
; reboot console
CALL BOOT_UP
```

DECLSN

Address: 0190h (EOS FD44h)

Without affecting the MSN, decrement the LSN of the byte pointed to by HL. HL remains the same

INPUT:

- HL = pointer to a byte value.

FUNCTION(S):

- Decrement low nibble (LSN) of a byte pointed to by HL without effecting the high nibble part (MSN).

OUTPUTS:

- (HL) = old MSN | new LSN Z flag set if decrement LSN results in 0, reset otherwise.
- Z flag set if decrement LSN results in 0, reset otherwise.
- C flag set if decrement LSN results in -1, reset otherwise

EXAMPLE:

```
LD  HL,OURVALUE
LD  A,$ff
LD  (HL),A
CALL  DECLSN
LD  A,(HL)
; A = $fe
```

DECMSN

Address: 019Bh (EOS FD47h)

Without affecting the LSN, decrement the MSN of the byte pointed to by HL. HL remains the same.

INPUT:

- HL = pointer to a byte value.

FUNCTION(S):

- Decrement high nibble (MSN) of a byte pointed to by HL without effecting the low nibble part (LSN).

OUTPUTS:

- (HL) = old LSN | new MSN Z flag set if decrement MSN results in 0, reset otherwise.
- Z flag set if decrement MSN results in 0, reset otherwise.
- C flag set if decrement MSN results in -1, reset otherwise

EXAMPLE:

```
LD  HL,OURVALUE
LD  A,$ff
LD  (HL),A
CALL  DECMSN
LD  A,(HL)
; A = $ef
```

DISPLAY_LOGO

Address: 1319h

Displays the ColecoVision logo screen with COLECOVISION on a black background.

If no cartridge is detected, a default message is displayed for 60^2 seconds, instructing the operator to turn the game off before inserting the cartridge or expansion module.

Otherwise, the game title, manufacturer, and copyright year are obtained from the cartridge and overlaid onto the logo screen for a period of 10^3 seconds before the game starts.

DISPLAY_LOGO exists with the VDP in mode II, the screen blanked, and the ASCII character set in VRAM.

VDP MEMORY MAP

The memory map is as follows:

Address Range	Description
3800H-3FFFH	Sprite pattern table
2000H-27FFH	Pattern colour table
1B00H-1B7FH	Sprite attribute table
1800H-1AFFH	Name table
0000H-17FFH	Pattern table

INPUT:

- None

FUNCTION(S):

- Clean up the 16K VRAM (0000h-4000h)
- Set default screen mode II by calling **MODE_1**
- Load default ASCII by calling **LOAD_ASCII**
- Load the logo pattern and put it on the screen, add tm beside the logo
- Put the year 1982, centred, at the bottom
- Load logo colours
- Enable display Test if a cartridge is present:
- 1. If it's present,
  - o   Add game information from cartridge to screen (title, company, year)
  - o   Wait 10 seconds - Turn off the display and start the game
- 2. Otherwise,
  - o   Display the default message for 60 seconds then turn off the display

OUTPUTS:

- None

---

[2] Original Coleco documented value – since measured to be ~75 seconds on all systems

[3] Average, varies by system region

```
; Display ColecoVision Logo
CALL DISPLAY_LOGO
```

MSNTOLSN

Address: 01A6 (EOS FD4Ah)

Copy MSN of the byte pointed to by HL to the LSN of that byte. HL remains the same.

INPUT:

- HL = pointer to a byte value.

FUNCTION(S):

- Copy high nibble (MSN) part of a byte value pointed to by HL to the low nibble part (LSN) of that byte.

OUTPUTS:

- (HL) = MSN | MSN

EXAMPLE:

```
LD  HL,OURVALUE
LD  A,$4f
LD  (HL),A
CALL MSNTOLSN
LD  A,(HL)
; A = $f4
```

POWER_UP

Address: 006Eh

Resets the sound channels, initialises the controllers and displays the ColecoVision logo.

INPUT:

- None

FUNCTION(S):

- Check for the presence of a game cartridge (at 08000h)
- If the cartridge ROM's first two bytes are 055h and 0AAh, then start the game immediately.
- Otherwise,
  - o Turn off sound channels
  - o Initialize pseudo-random number generator
  - o Initialize controller to strobe reset
  - o Set no deferred writes to VRAM
  - o Set no sprites multiplexing
  - o Continuing the execution by displaying the logo screen

OUTPUTS:

- None

EXAMPLE:

```
; restart the console
CALL POWER_UP
```

RAND_GEN

Address: 1FFDh

Generates the next pseudo-random number.

INPUT:

- None

FUNCTION(S):

- Set of bit operations on **RAND_NUM** to calculate the next pseudo-random value.

OUTPUTS:

- HL = (RAND_NUM)
- A = L

EXAMPLE:

```
; get the next random number
CALL RAND_GEN
```

Appendix B – Adam Computer EOS

If you target your game to either exclusively run on an Adam Computer or just to support the extra features available, then the Adam provides a set of additional BIOS functions called the 'Elementary Operating System' (EOS).

EOS Initialisation

If your title loads from Adam digital tape or floppy disc, the EOS functions will already be available to use at the high RAM location starting at E000h-F3FFh. They are copied there as part of the boot-up process.

But if it is a cartridge, you will need to select the EOS into the lower bank (see Memory Bank Switch Port (7fh)) and copy the EOS functions to E000h as follows:

```
; Strobe the EOS_ENABLE line by writing the value 02h to port 3Fh
out $3f,$02
; Copy EOS from location 6000h to location E000h
ld hl,$6000
ld de,$e000
ld bc,($FEC0 - $E000)
ldir
; Deselect EOS ROM
out $3f,0
; Initialise EOS tbales. All RAM should be cleared to 0.
ld bc,CLEAR_RAM_SIZE
ld de,CLEAR_RAM_START + 1
ld hl,CLEAR_RAM_START
xor a
ld (hl),a
ldir
; Initialise I/O ports
CALL PORT_COLLECTION
; Initialise AdamNet
CALL _HARD_INIT
```

EOS Memory Map

EOS uses some defined blocks of memory in the upper 32k of in-built RAM as follows:

Description	Memory Range
File Control Block Headers	D390h-D3FFh
FCB Buffers (3 x 1k)	D400h-DFFFh
EOS Code (copied from ROM on startup)	E000h-F3FFh
AdamNet Device Drivers	F400H-FBFFh
EOS Data Tables	FC00h-FC2Fh
EOS Jump Tables	FC30h-FD4Fh
Global RAM Area	FD50h-FEBFh
Processor Control Block	FEC0h-FEC3h
Device Control Block	FEC4h-FFFEh
DMA Reserved Byte	FFFFh

EOS Error Codes

Error	Value
DCB_NOT_FOUND	1
DCB_BUSY	2
DCB_IDLE_ERR	3
NO_DATE_ERR	4
NO_FILE_ERR	5
FILE_EXISTS_ERR	6
NO_FCB_ERR	7
MATCH_ERR	8
BAD_FNUM_ERR	9
EOF_ERR	10
TOO_BIG_ERR	11
FULL_DIR_ERR	12
FULL_TAPE_ERR	13
FILE_NM_ERR	14
RENAME_ERR	15
DELETE_ERR	16
RANGE_ERR	17
CANT_SYNC1	18
CANT_SYNC2	19
PRT_ERR	20
RQ_TP_STATE_ERR	21
DEVICE_DEPD_ERR	22
PROG_NON_EXIST	23
NO_DIR_ERR	24

EOS Functions

Several of the OS7 ROM routines are also available at a location in the EOS functions, so the EOS address of a repeated function will be shown in the OS 7 section, Appendix A – ColecoVision BIOS Functions (OS 7).

As this book's primary goal is about developing games, the remainder of the EOS functions are included here for completeness, but their use will need to be covered in a future volume.

System Operations

_EOS_START

Address: FC30h

Starts EOS by going through initialisation steps.

INPUT:

- None

OUTPUTS:

- B = Boot device number

_FIND_DCB

Address: FC54h

Find the DCB address for the assigned device.

INPUT:

- A = Device

OUTPUTS:

- Zero Flag Set = No Error
- A = Device ID or Error code
- IY = Pointer to DCB for selected device or garbage if an error

_GET_DCB_ADDR

Address: FC57h

Same as _FIND_DCB.

INPUT:

- A = Device

OUTPUTS:

- Zero Flag Set = No Error
- A = Device ID or Error code
- IY = Pointer to DCB for selected device or garbage if an error

_GET_PCB_ADDR

Address: FC5Ah

Finds the current PCB address of the system.

INPUT:

- None

OUTPUTS:

- IY = Current PCB address

_HARD_INIT

Address: FC5Dh

Initialises the system at powerup

INPUT:

- None

OUTPUTS:

- None

_HARD_RESET_NET

Address: FC60h

Applies hardware reset (38h) to AdamNet.

INPUT:

- None

OUTPUTS:

- None

PORT_COLLECTION

Address: FD11h

Initialise I/O ports. EOS collects port values from the OS_7 ROM. EOS routines use these ports when the access the video processor, controllers and sound generator.

INPUT:

- None

OUTPUTS:

- None

_RELOC_PCB

Address: FC78h

Relocates PCB and CBSs to different addresses after powerup if necessary.

INPUT:

- HL = Address to relocate PCB to

OUTPUT:

- A = 83h, zero flag set

_REQUEST_STATUS

Address: FC7Eh

Issues a status request command to a device.

INPUT:

- A = Device

OUTPUTS:

- Zero Flag Set = No Errors
- A = Error code if non-zero
- IT = DCB address or garbage if DCB not found

_SCAN_ACTIVE

Address: FC8Ah

Scans for devices on AdamNet and establishes the Device Control Blocks (DCB).

INPUT:

- The PCB must be set

OUTPUTS:

- None

_SOFT_INIT

Address: FC8Dh

Initialises the system anytime but powerup.

INPUT:

- HL = New PCB Address

OUTPUTS:

- None

_SYNC

Address: FCB1h

Synchronises Z80 with Master 6801.

- None

- Zero flag indicates success, A = error code if non-zero

Simple Device Operations

_CONS_INIT

Address: FC36h

Initialises the system console setting up a window for screen display.

INPUT:

- B = number of columns (0 to31)
- C = number of lines (0 to 23)
- D = Home column
- E = Home row
- HL = Pointer to pattern name table

OUTPUTS:

- None

_CONS_OUT

Address: FC39h

Displays a character or performs screen control on the system console.

If A equals one of the following values a specific action is performed:

Value	Key	Description
08	Backspace	Move the cursor left one
0A	^J	Move cursor down one line (line feed)
0C	^L	Clear screen and home cursor
0D	Return	Return cursor to start of line (must send line feed if new line wanted)
16	^V	Delete to the end of the line
18	^X	Delete to the end of the screen
1C	^\	Place cursor at position DE
80	Home	Home the cursor (no clear)
A0	Up Arrow	Move up
A1	Right Arrow	Move right
A2	Down Arrow	Move down
A3	Left Arrow	Move left

INPUT:

- A = Character to print or Place Cursor request
- D = Column to go to if Place Cursor request
- E = Row to go to if Place Cursor request

OUPUTS:

- None

_CONS_DISP

Address: FC33h

Outputs a single character to the console window.

INPUT:

A = Character to display

OUTPUTS:

None

_REQ_KBD_STAT

Address: FC81h

Requests keyboard status.

INPUT:

- None

OUTPUTS:

- Zero Flag Set = No Errors, A = Error code if non-zero
- IY = Address of DCB

_REQ_PR_STAT

Address: FC84h

Requests printer status.

INPUT:

- None

OUTPUT:

- Zero flag set = read, otherwise A = Error Code
- IY = Address of DCB

_RD_DEV_DEP_STA

Address: FCE4h

Gets the device-specific status which was reported during the _REQUEST_STATUS.

INPUT:

- A = Device

OUTPUTS:

- Zero Flag Set = No Errors
- A = Error code if non-zero OR status value

_RD_KBD

Address: FC6Ch

Reads a character from the keyboard.

INPUT:

- None

OUTPUTS:

- Zero Flag Set = No Error
- A = Character if no error, otherwise the error code

_START_RD_CH_DEV

Address: FCA5h

Sets up a character device DCB to issue read command (concurrent operation).

INPUT:

- A = Device

OUTPUTS:

- Zero Flag Set = Successful
- A = Error Code if non-zero

_END_RD_CH_DEV

Address: FC48h

Checks the status of the character device DCB after a command has been sent to read (concurrent).

INPUT:

- None

OUTPUTS:

- No Carry = No character waiting
- Carry Set = Character (if no error), A = Character
- Zero Flag Set = No Error, A = Error code if non-zero

_START_RD_KBD

Address: FCA8h

Starts a keyboard read command (concurrent).

INPUT:

- None

OUTPUTS:

- Zero Flag Set = Successful
- A = Error Code if non-zero

_END_RD_KBD

Address: FC4Bh

Check the keyboard status (concurrent).

INPUT:

- None

OUTPUTS:

- No Carry = No character waiting
- Carry Set = Character (if no error), A = Character
- Zero Flag Set = No Error, A = Error code if non-zero

_WR_CH_DEV

Address: FC87h

Initiates a write command to a character device.

_PR_BUFF

Address: FC63h

Prints a string of ASCII characters terminated by ETX (03).

INPUT:

- HL = Pointer to the start of the string to print

OUTPUT:

- Zero flag set = successful, otherwise A = Error Code

_PR_CH

Address: FC66h

Prints a character on the printer.

INPUT:

- A = Character to print

OUTPUT:

- Zero flag set = successful, otherwise A = Error Code

_START_WR_CH_DEV

Address: FCA5h

Sets up a character device DCB to issue a write command (DCB).

INPUT:

- A = Character to print

OUTPUT:

- Zero flag set = successful, otherwise A = Error Code

_END_WR_CH_DEV

Address: FC51h

Checks the status of character device DCB after the command has been sent to write (concurrent).

_START_PR_BUFF

Address: FC9Ch

Starts the command of printing a string of characters (concurrent).

INPUT:

- HL = Address of string to send to the printer, terminated with ASCII 03.

OUTPUT:

- Zero flag set = successful, otherwise A = Error Code

_END_PR_BUFF

Address: FC3Fh

Check the printer status (concurrent).

INPUT:

- None

OUTPUTS:

- Carry set = Completed
- No Carry and Zero = Not Completed
- Non-Zero = Error and A = Error Code

_START_PR_CH

Address: FC9Fh

Starts a printer print command (concurrent).

INPUT:

- A = Character to print

OUTPUT:

- Zero flag set = successful, otherwise A = Error Code

_END_PR_CH

Address: FC42h

Check the printer status (concurrent).

INPUT:

- None

OUTPUTS:

- Carry set = Completed
- No Carry and Zero = Not Completed
- Non-Zero = Error and A = Error Code

_SOFT_RES_DEV

Address: FC90h

Used to reset a device back to its default state.

INPUT:

- A = Device

OUTPUTS:

- Zero Flag Set = Success
- A = Error code if non-zero OR 128 if complete

_SOFT_RES_KBD

Address: FC93h

Resets the keyboard to its default state.

INPUT:

- None

OUTPUTS:

- Zero Flag Set = Success
- A = Error code if non-zero

_SOFT_RES_PR

Address: FC96h

Resets the printer to its default state.

INPUT:

- None

OUTPUTS:

- Zero Flag Set = Success
- A = Error code if non-zero

File Manager Operations

_SET_DATE

Address: FCD8h

Sets the current date.

INPUT:

- B = Day
- C = Month
- D = Year

OUTPUT:

- None

_GET_DATE

Address: FCDBh

Gets the current date.

INPUT:

- None

OUTPUTS:

- Zero Flag Set = Success
- A = Error code if non-zero
- B = Day in Binary Coded Decimal (BCD)
- C = Month
- D = Year

_CHECK_FCB

Address: FCF0h

Finds a file matching the supplied name, in the 2nd and 3rd file control blocks (FCB).

INPUT:

- HL = Address of the file name

OUTPUTS:

- Zero Flag Set = File found, A = Error Code if non-zero
- A = FCB number if found
- B = File Mode if found
- HL = Points to file control block (FCB) if found

_DELETE_FILE

Address: FCE1h

Remove a file from the directory.

INPUT:

- A = Device
- HL = Address of file name

OUTPUT:

- Zero Flag Set = Success
- A = Error code if non-zero

_MODE_CHECK

Address: FCF9h

Check the file mode in the FCB is within range.

INPUT:

- HL = Directory entry
- IX = Pointer to FCB

OUTPUTS:

- Zero Flag Set = Ok, A = Error code if non-zero

_QUERY_FILE

Address: FCCCh

Reads directory entry of a file.

INPUT:

- A = Device
- DE = Pointer to the file name
- HL = Pointer to user buffer

OUTPUTS:

- Zero Flag Set = File found, A = Error code if non-zero
- BC/DE = File start block if found
- (HL) = Directory entry if found

_SET_FILE

Address: FCCFh

Updates the file directory entry.

INPUT:

- A = Device
- DE = Address of file name
- HL = Address of user File Control Block (FCB)

OUTPUTS:

- Zero Flag Set = No Error, A = Error code if non-zero

_MAKE_FILE

Address: FCC9h

Creates a file in the directory.

Note: It does not write any data to the file itself.

INPUT:

- A = Device
- BC & DE = File size in bytes
- HL = Pointer to file name

OUTPUTS:

- Zero Flag Set = Success, A= Error code if non-zero

_OPEN_FILE

Address: FCC0h

Opens a file by setting up the FCB.

INPUT:

- A = Device
- B = Mode
- HL = Address of file name

OUTPUTS:

- Zero Flag Set = No error
- A = File number or Error Code
- B = File number if no error

_CLOSE_FILE

Address: FCC3h

Closes a file by marking the FCB.

INPUT:

- A = File number

OUTPUTS:

- Zero Flag Set = Successful
- A = Error code if non-zero

_INIT_TAPE_DIR

Address: FCBDh

Initialises a directory and clears the block allocations.

INPUT:

- A = Device
- C = Number of K in directory
- DE = Size of medium (160K, 256K, 320K etc)
- HL = Volume name

OUTPUTS:

- Zero Flag Set = No Error
- A = Error code if non-zero

_RENAME_FILE

Address: FCDEh

Change a files name.

INPUT:

- A = Device
- DE = Address of old name
- HL = Address of new name

OUTPUTS:

- Zero Flag Set = Success
- A = Error code if non-zero

_RESET_FILE

Address: FCC6h

Resets the file by pointing back to the first byte.

INPUT:

- A = File number

OUTPUTS:

- Zero Flag Set = Success
- A = Error code if non-zero

_READ_FILE

Address: FCD2h

Reads data from a file into user supplied buffer.

INPUT:

- A = File number
- BC = Number of bytes required
- HL = Address to user buffer to store bytes

OUTPUTS:

- Zero Flag Set = Success
- A = Error code if non-zero
- BC = Number of bytes transferred

_WRITE_FILE

Address: FCD5h

Writes data to a file from a user supplied buffer.

INPUT:

- A = File Number
- BC = Bytes to write
- HL = Address of bytes to write

OUTPUTS:

- Zero Flag Set = Success
- A = Error code if non-zero

_FMGR_INIT

Address: FCBAh

Initialises the File Manager.

INPUT:

- DE = Pointer to 3k of memory for FCB transfer buffers
- HL = Pointer to 105 bytes for three File Control Blocks (FCB).

OUTPUTS:

- None

_SCAN_FOR_FILE

Address: FCFCh

Scans the directory block(s) for a file.

INPUT:

- HL = Pointer to a file name

OUTPUTS:

- Zero Flag Set = File found, A = Error Code if non-zero
- BC/DE = Start block of file if found

_TRIM_FILE

Address: FCEDh

Sets the file size as the actual size of the file if the size allocated in the directory is larger.

INPUT:

- A = Device
- DE = Address of file name

OUTPUTS:

- Zero Flag Set = No Errors
- A = Error code if non-zero

Device Driver Operations

_READ_BLOCK

Address: FCF3h

Reads a block of data from a device, includes error handling and will retry up to twice to complete the request.

INPUT:

- A = Device
- BCDE = Block number
- HL = Address of destination buffer

OUTPUTS:

- Zero Flag Set = Success
- A = Error code if non-zero

_RD_1_BLOCK

Address: FC69h

Reads a block of data (1024 bytes) from a mass storage device and aborts on error.

INPUT:

- A = Device
- BCDE = Block number
- HL = Address of destination buffer

OUTPUTS:

- Zero Flag Set = Success
- A = Error code if non-zero

_WRITE_BLOCK

Address: FCF6h

Writes a block of data to a device, includes errors handling and will retry up to twice to complete the request.

INPUTS:

- A = Device
- BCDE = Block number
- HL = Address where source data is located

OUTPUTS:

- Zero Flag Set = Success
- A = Error code if non-zero

_WR_1_BLOCK

Address: FC84h

Writes a block of data to a mass storage device. I/O buffers containing data to be transferred to tape can reside anywhere in Z80 RAM.

INPUTS:

- A = Device
- BCDE = Block number
- HL = Address where source data is located

OUTPUTS:

- Zero Flag Set = Success
- A = Error code if non-zero

_REQ_TAPE_STAT

Address: FC87h

Requests status of the data pack drive.

_START_RD_1_BLOCK

Address: FCA2h

Sends read command to read a block of data from a block device (concurrent).

INPUT:

- A = Device
- BCDE = Block number
- HL = Address of destination buffer

OUTPUTS:

- Zero Flag Set = Success
- A = Error code if non-zero

_END_RD_1_BLOCK

Address: FC45h

Checks status after _START_RD_1_BLOCK.

INPUT:

- A = Device

OUTPUTS:

- Carry Flag Set = Complete
- Zero Flag Set = No Error if Carry Set
- A = Error Code if non-zero

_START_WR_1_BLOCK

Address: FCA2h

Sends write command to write a block of data to a block device (concurrent).

INPUTS:

- A = Device
- BCDE = Block number
- HL = Address where source data is located

OUTPUTS:

- Zero Flag Set = Success
- A = Error code if non-zero

_END_WR_1_BLOCK

Address: FC4Eh

Checks status after

_START_WR_1_BLOCK.

INPUT:

- A = Device

OUTPUTS:

- Carry Flag Set = Complete
- Zero Flag Set = No Error if Carry Set
- A = Error Code if non-zero

Appendix C – Memory Map

Memory Maps

The ColecoVision and the Adam have slightly different memory maps: with the ColecoVision only having 1K of RAM versus the Adam having a full 32K.

ColecoVision General Memory Map

ADDRESS	Description
0000-1FFF	ColecoVision BIOS OS 7'
2000-5FFF	Expansion port
6000-7FFF	1K RAM mapped into 8K. (7000-73FF)
8000-FFFF	Game cartridge

Adam General Memory Map

ADDRESS	Description
0000-1FFF	ColecoVision BIOS OS 7'/ Lower 8K of RAM
2000-7FFF	24K RAM. (2000-73FF)
8000-FFFF	Game cartridge/Upper 32K RAM

Complete OS 7' RAM Map

The ColecoVision BIOS routines have several RAM locations reserved for their use. In addition, the Z80 stack, which is used to remember return locations from CALLs and by the programmer to store values also needs to be considered.

ADDRESS	NAME	DESCRIPTION
7000-701F		Usable RAM, every byte counts, plus if you don't use the OS sound routines you can use the next 9 bytes as well.
7020-7021	PTR_LST_OF_SND_ADDRS	Pointer to list (in RAM) of sound addresses
7022-7023	PTR_TO_S_ON_0	Pointer to song for noise
7024-7025	PTR_TO_S_ON_1	Pointer to song for channel#1
7026-7027	PTR_TO_S_ON_2	Pointer to song for channel#2
7028-7029	PTR_TO_S_ON_3	Pointer to song for channel#3
702A	SAVE_CTRL	CTRL data (byte)
702B-		This is a usable area of RAM for your application to use but be mindful of running into the stack.
73B9	STACK	This is the TOP of the stack; it will expand down from its starting address, so you need to make sure you leave some room for it to grow.
73BA-73BF	PARAM_AREA	Common passing parameters area (PASCAL). If you are not using the Pascal entry points can of course be used.
73C0-73C1	TIMER_LENGTH	Length of timer
73C2	TEST_SIG_NUM	Signal Code
73C3-73C4	VDP_MODE_WORD	The VDP mode word contains a copy of the data in the 1st two VDP registers. By examining this data, the OS and cartridge programs can make mode-dependent decisions about the sprite size or VRAM table arrangement. This word is updated by the WRITE_REGISTER routine whenever the contents of registers 0 or 1 are changed
73C5	VDP_STATUS_BYTE	The default handler for the NMI, which must read the VDP status register to clear the interrupt condition, places the VDP contents here. This byte is the most accurate representation of the actual VDP status that is available to the cartridge programmer, provided the VDP interrupt is enabled on-chip.
73C6	DEFER_WRITES	This is a Boolean flag which is set to FALSE at power-up time and should be set to TRUE only if the cartridge programmer wishes to defer writes to VRAM. If this flag is TRUE, then the WRITER routine must be called regularly to perform deferred writes.

73C7	MUX_SPRITES	This Boolean flag with default FALSE value should be set to TRUE if the cartridge programmer wishes one level of indirection to be inserted into sprite processing by having all sprites written to a local SPRITE_NAME_TABLE before being written to VRAM. This aids sprite multiplexing solutions to the 5th sprite on a line problem.
73C8-73C9	RAND_NUM	This is the shift register used by the random number generator. It is initialised at power-up.
73CA	QUEUE_SIZE	This is the size of the deferred write queue. It is set by the cartridge programmer. It has a range 0 – 255.
73CB	QUEUE_HEAD	Index of the head of the write queue
73CC	QUEUE_TAIL	Index of the tail of the write queue
73CD-73CE	HEAD_ADDRESS	Address of the queue head
73CF-73D0	TAIL_ADDRESS	Address of the queue tail
73D1-73D2	BUFFER	This is a pointer to the beginning of the deferred write queue. The cartridge programmer is responsible for providing a RAM area to hold the queue and passing its location and size to INIT_QUEUE.
73D3-73D4	TIMER_TABLE_BASE	Timer base address
73D5-73D6	NEXT_TIMER_DATA_BYTE	The next available timer address
73D7-73EA	DBNCE_BUFF	Debounce buffer. 5 pairs (old and state) of fire, joy, spin, arm, and keyboard for each player.
73EB	SPIN_SW0_CT	Spinner counter port#1
73EC	SPIN_SW1_CT	Spinner counter port#2
73ED	-	(reserved)
73EE	S0_C0	Segment 0 data, Controller port #1
73EF	S0_C1	Segment 0 data, Controller port #2
73F0	S1_C0	Segment 1 data, Controller port #1
73F1	S1_C1	Segment 1 data, Controller port #2
73F2-73FB	VRAM_ADDR_TABLE	Block of VRAM table pointers
73F2-73F3	SPRITENAMETBL	Sprite name table offset
73F4-73F5	SPRITEGENTBL	Sprite generator table offset
73F6-73F7	PATTERNNAMETBL	Pattern name table offset
73F8-73F9	PATTERNGENTBL	Pattern generator table offset
73FA-73FB	COLORTABLE	Colour table offset
73FC-73FD	SAVE_TEMP	(not used in VRAM routines)
73FE-73FF	SAVED_COUNT	Copy of COUNT for PUT_VRAM & GET_VRAM

Appendix D – Z80 I/O Ports Assignments

ColecoVision Console

These are the common I/O ports used by the ColecoVision and Adam Computer.

Video Display Processor

Data port	0BEH
Register port	0BFH

Sound Generator

Data port	0FFH (write-only)

Game Controller

Strobe Set port	080H (write-only)
Strobe Reset port	0C0H (write-only)
Controller#1 port	0FCH (read-only)
Controller#2 port	0FFH (read-only)

Modem

Data port	05EH
Control port	05FH
Auto Dialler	01EH

Expansion connector #2

Data port	04FH

Memory Map

Control port	07FH

Network reset

03FH (Performed by setting and resetting bit 0)

EOS enable	03FH (Performed by setting bit 1)
EOS disable	03FH (Performed by resetting bit 1)

Adam Computer

The Adam Computer has a much larger port map due to having a larger number of peripheral devices

Port #	Device	Input	Output
00	Powermate SASI Hard Drive	Input Data	Output Data
01	Powermate SASI Hard Drive	Status Register	Command Register
01	MIB2 RESET line	* Not Used on MIB2 *	Bit 3 = 1 for MIB2 RESET
01	Powermate IDE Hard Drive	Error Register	* Not Used on IDE HD *
02	Powermate IDE Hard Drive	Sector Count Register	Sector Count Register
03	Powermate IDE Hard Drive	Sector Number Register	Sector Number Register
04	Powermate IDE Hard Drive	Cylinder Low Register	Cylinder Low Register
05	Powermate IDE Hard Drive	Cylinder High Register	Cylinder High Register
06	Powermate IDE Hard Drive	SDH Register	SDH Register
07	Powermate IDE Hard Drive	Status Register	Command Register
08	Bonafide Sys MIDI Interface		
09	Bonafide Sys MIDI Interface		
0A	Bonafide Sys MIDI Interface		
0B	Bonafide Sys MIDI Interface		
0C	Bonafide Sys MIDI Interface		
0D	Bonafide Sys MIDI Interface		
0E	Bonafide Sys MIDI Interface		
0F	Bonafide Sys MIDI Interface		
10	Powermate Serial ports	Mode Register A	Mode Register A
11	Powermate Serial ports	Status Register A	Clock Select Reg A
12	Powermate Serial ports	* DO NOT USE *	Command Register A
13	Powermate Serial ports	RX Holding Register A	TX Holding Reg A
14	Powermate Serial ports	Input Port Change Reg	Aux Control Register
15	Powermate Serial ports	Interrupt Status Reg	Interrupt Mask Reg
16	Powermate Serial ports	Read Counter Upper	Set C/T Upper Register
17	Powermate Serial ports	Read Counter Lower	Set C/T Lower Register
18	Powermate Serial ports	Mode Register B	Mode Register B
19	Powermate Serial ports	Status Register B	Clock Select Reg B
1A	Powermate Serial ports	* DO NOT USE *	Command Register B
1B	Powermate Serial ports	RX Holding Register B	TX Holding Register B

1C	Powermate Serial ports	* Reserved (note 5) *	MIB3 Serial Port RESET
1D	Powermate Serial ports	Read Input Port Bits	Output Port Config Reg
1E	Coleco AutoDialer	??	??
1E	Powermate Serial ports	Start Counter Cmd Port	Set Output Port Bits
1F	Powermate Serial ports	Stop Counter Cmd Port	Reset Output Port Bits
20-3F	AdamNet Reset	Input MAY be available	Output is NOT available
40	Parallel Printer interface	Printer status	Output Data
41	Maybe unused (see note 1)	Input may NOT be avail	Output MAY be available
42	Expansion Memory	* Not Used *	Bank Number
43	Maybe unused (see note 1)	Input may NOT be avail	Output MAY be available
44-47	Eve/Orphanware Serial Port		
48-4B	Eve Speech Synth/Clock Card		
4C-4F	Orphanware Serial Port 2	(Standard Eve 80 column terminal ports)	
4F	Coleco Steering controller	(Listed in Hackers guide as Expansion conn #2)	
50-53	*** Unused ***		
54-57	Orphanware Serial Port 3	(Standard Orphanware 80 column terminal ports)	
58	Powermate IDE Hard Disk	Input Data Lower 8 bits	Output Data Lower 8 bits
59	Powermate IDE Hard Disk	Input Data Upper 8 bits	Output Data Upper 8 bits
5A	Powermate IDE Hard Disk	Alternate Status Reg	Fixed Disk Control Reg
5B	Powermate IDE Hard Disk	Digital Input Register	** Not Used by IDE HD **
5C-5F	Orphanware Serial Port 4		
5E	Adamlink Modem	Input Data	Output Data
5F	Adamlink Modem	Status	Control
60-7F	Memory Bank Switch Port	Input MAY be available	Output is NOT available
80-8F	*** Unused ***	(see note 2)	STA (?)

90-9F	Orphanware Hard Drive		STA (?)
A0-BF	Video Display Processor		
C0	Strobe Reset		STB (?)
C1-DF	*** Unused ***	(see note 2)	STB (?)
E0-FF	Sound Chip (Out only)		
FC	Joystick #1 (In only)		
FE	Joystick #2 (In only)		

Notes:

1. Port 41 or port 43 is used by the Eve 80 column unit as a keyboard input port.
2. Not useable from expansion card slots (can't read or write data to or from ports) - may be available on side port.
3. Powermate IDE hard disk drive will not interfere with Powermate serial ports.
4. Powermate serial ports will probably interfere with the auto dialler.
5. Reserved ports in Powermate serial port map: Input ports 12 and 1A - screw up serial ports if used; Input port 1C doesn't bother anything but the 2681 drives the bus.
6. Orphanware serial port number 4 probably interferes with the Adamlink modem.

Memory Bank Switch Port (7fh)

The Adam Computer comes with:

- 64K of CPU RAM (as well as 16K of Video RAM),
- OS 7 ROM (the same as the ColecoVision) and
- SmartWRITER ROM and EOS ROM

Unfortunately, the Z80 can only access 64K of memory at any one time, so all the above parts can't be available at the same time.

To get around this, you can select combinations of the parts by sending a single byte to port 7fh as follows:

Lower Memory Option Selection

Bits 0 and 1 control the lower 32K of memory and can be set to:

D0	D1	Description
0	0	SmartWRITER ROM and EOS ROM
0	1	32K Inbuilt RAM
1	0	32K Expansion RAM
1	1	OS7 + 24K Inbuilt RAM

Upper Memory Option Selection

Bits 2 and 3 control the upper 32K of memory and can be set to:

D2	D3	Description
0	0	32K Inbuilt RAM
0	1	Expansion ROM
1	0	Expansion RAM
1	1	Cartridge ROM

Note: Bits 4-7 are reserved for future expansion and should always be set to 0.

Appendix E – Distributing Your Title

Writing a software title and sending the ROM file to other users to try out can be one goal, but it is even better to be able to release your hard work in physical cartridge form or perhaps a high-speed digital tape (for Adam users).

There are several paths you can follow, which will depend on the amount of space you need for your game code and data, and the intended audience for your title.

Standard Cartridges

A standard ColecoVision cartridge can be from 8 to 32K in size, which is ample space to be able to deliver many arcade-like games.

The cartridge layout is very simple, with a single EPROM chip of the appropriate size, a single capacitor and depending on the design, a small logic chip.

Figure 31 - R2Tronik ColecoVision Cartridge PCB

A standard ColecoVision cartridge requires no special techniques to construct your title, your game code just resides in a single block of up to 32K of ROM, starting at 08000h.

When your cartridge is plugged into a ColecoVision or Adam computer, the OS will jump straight to your code starting at 08000h.

At the time of printing, there were several cartridge PCBs available to programmers as follows:

- R2Tronik – ColecoVision Replacement PCB (32K)
  https://www.r2tronik.com/en/cartmodding/126-colecovision-replacement-pcb-for-repairprototyping-test-or-cart-modding-0715235390948.html
- Homebrews & more – 16K PCB Schematics
  http://buzz.computer.free.fr/index.php?post/2012/12/11/ColecoVision-single-ROM-Cartridge
- ColecoVision Homebrew Kit (32K with shell and all components)
  http://www.colecovision.eu/ColecoVision/development/Homebrew%20kit%20CV.shtml
- The ColecoVision Addict web site has a Creation section with details on making your own cartridge PCBs
  https://cvaddict.com/article.php?articleid=24

MegaCart

The MegaCart is a special design (originally by Bryan Edward) that allows ROMs to contain up to 1MB if required.

The cartridge can be several different sizes as follows:

- 128K - 8 banks of 16K
- 256K - 16 banks of 16K
- 512K - 32 banks of 16K
- 1MB - 64 banks of 16K

The first 16K of ROM is fixed to the last 16k section of the ROM and is located at 8000h to BFFFh on the ColecoVision (and Adam).

The 2nd 16K area (C000h to FFFFh) can be changed to any of the banks in the cartridge (including the last one) by reading from memory address FFC0h to FFFFh i.e. each location represents one of the 64 possible memory banks to select.

This also means, depending on the size of the ROM, that the top 8 to 64 bytes (FFC0h to FFFFh) of each 16K ROM bank can't be used.

Example Usage (from MegaCart documentation):

```
; For 128K Megacart (for 256K one I start on $fff0 up
; to SLOT_15 at $ffff)
SLOT_0: equ $fff8
SLOT_1: equ $fff9
SLOT_2: equ $fffa
SLOT_3: equ $fffb
SLOT_4: equ $fffc
SLOT_5: equ $fffd
SLOT_6: equ $fffe
SLOT_7: equ $ffff
; At start of code
ld hl,SLOT_0 ; Default slot of Megacart,
; but set again because user can do a ColecoVision RESET
call sel_slot
; My typical switching code
ld hl,SLOT_3
call sel_slot
; Slot selection
sel_slot:
ld (slot),hl ; Saves current slot, useful because in NMI
; routine sometimes I switch slots to play music from OTHER slot
ld a,(hl)
ret
```

More details of how to build a MegaCart are available on the ColecoVision Addict web site: https://cvaddict.com/article.php?articleid=27

High-Speed Tape

With the Adam Computer you can of course still use a standard cartridge or MegaCart but due to all Adam's coming with at least one High-Speed Tape drive, you can also distribute your title on digital tape.

This allows your title to be up to 256K in size if you are prepared to load in more parts of the title into Adam's larger RAM storage as you need them from the tape.

Loading a title from tape involves a bit more setup and preparation of your game code.

If you start an Adam Computer with no cartridge, it will look for any connected disc drives with media. If none are found it will check each of the possible two digital tape drives for the presence of a tape, and then load the first data block (block 0) from the tape into memory at C800h.

Each block is 1K in size so, your first block needs to load the rest of your title into memory from the tape (as required).

Appendix F – Text editor setup guide

Setup Visual Studio Code

Step 1 – Setting up the text editor

Download and install

Download Visual Studio Code from https://code.visualstudio.com and install it using the default settings.

Setting up Z80 Syntax Highlighting

Next, to make our Z80 assembler code more readable, we need to add a highlighter extension that will colour the different parts of our assemble code. This makes it much easier to read and see what is going on in our code.

Either press the Extensions icon

or press Ctrl + Shift + X and then type "Z80 Macro", then extension called "Z80 Macro-Assembler" by mborik should be near the top of the list. Click on it and press the [Install] button and it will be added to your Visual Studio installation.

Step 2 – Setting up the Z80 Assembler

Next, we need to set up the Z80 Assembler.

Download the freely available version of the Z80 Assembler by TNI (since the 1st edition was published, the TNI website has gone offline, I have hosted a copy on my website instead) and unzip it to the following directory:

C:\tniasm045

Inside the directory you should see the following files:

- tniasm.exe
- tniasm.txt

It is a great, free Z80 assembler with lots of features. The 1.0 version will be released at some stage, so show your interest by sending an email to the current developers.

Running the Assembler

Open a new Terminal window, and type: `.\make.bat` and press [Enter].

Setup ConTEXT

Step 1 – Setting up the text editor

Download and Install

Download ConTEXT and then install using the default settings.

Setting up Z80 Syntax Highlighting

Next, to make our Z80 assembly code more readable, we need to add a highlighter file that will colour the different parts of our assembly code. This makes it much easier to read and see what is going on in our code.

Download the "WLA DX Z80 Assembler.chl" file and put it in the following directory:

```
C:\Program Files (x86)\ConTEXT\Highlighters
```

This directory will be the following if you have a 32-bit version of Windows:

```
C:\Program Files\ConTEXT\Highlighters
```

Step 2 – Setting up the Z80 Assembler

Next, we need to set up the Z80 Assembler.

Download the freely available version of the Z80 Assembler by TNI (since the 1st edition was published, the TNI website has gone offline, I have hosted a copy on my website instead) and unzip it to the following directory:

C:\tniasm045

Inside the directory you should see the following files:

- tniasm.exe
- tniasm.txt

It is a great, free Z80 assembler with lots of features. The 1.0 version will be released at some stage, so show your interest by sending an email to the current developers.

Step 3 – Add an execute key to ConTEXT for the Assembler

To make things easier while editing and debugging our Z80 code using ConTEXT you can add an 'Execute Key' to compile the currently open file using the TNI Assembler, and most importantly, show any errors from the compile output, which you can then use to jump to the error line.

Open an assembler source file, e.g. Template.asm, in the ColecoVision templates.

Go to [Options] from the top menu and select 'Environment Options'

Click on the 'Execute Keys' tab and you should see the following screen:

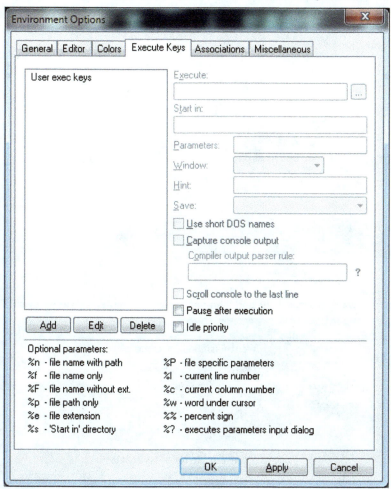

Then click on the 'Add' button and you should see the following screen:

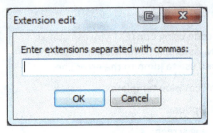

Figure 33 - ConTEXT - extension edit

Enter 'asm,z80' (don't type the quotes) and press [OK]

On the left you should now see:

Figure 34 - ConTEXT - Select execute key to define

Click on the function key you want to use, e.g. F9, and then on the right, fill in the fields as follows:

Field	Value to Enter
Execute	c:\tniasm045\tniasm.exe
Start in	%p
Parameters	%n
Window	Normal
Hint	Compile
Save	Current file before execution
Use short DOS names	Not ticked
Capture console output	Ticked
Compiler output parser rule	*line %l(%n)*
Scroll console to the last line	Ticked

Afterwards your screen should look like the following:

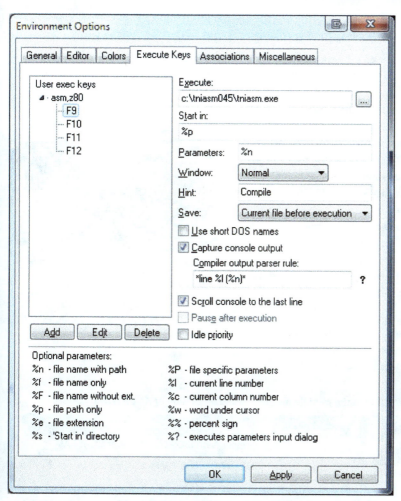

Figure 35 - ConTEXT – Execute keys setup

Once you press [OK] you can type the Execute key you selected, and the current file will be compiled with the output shown in a window at the bottom of the program.

Appendix G – Opcode Games Super Game Module

The Super Game Module is an expansion module for both the ColecoVision and Adam, released by Opcode Games in 2012, that adds two very important things that can extend what is possible on both systems as follows:

- Expands the CPU Ram from 1k up to a massive 32k
  - This allows for storage of more dynamic game assets, screen and music buffers.
- Adds an AY-3-8910 sound processor, the same as used in many arcade games as well as home computers, such as all MSX, Atari ST, Spectrum, Amstrad and many more.
  - The AY sound chip is a lot more capable than the Coleco's inbuilt SN sound chip, not only having greater frequency and volume range, but it also has inbuilt waveform control as well as channel mixing.

Figure 36 - Opcode Games Super Game Module

Multiple batches of the module have been released since 2013, so there are quite a few modules out there is active use, making it worthwhile to target your game, especially if the additional memory and sound capabilities would enhance your game.

Memory Map

The adjusted memory map with the module installed in a ColecoVision or Adam is as follows:

ADDRESS	Description
0000-1FFF	ColecoVision BIOS OS 7'/ Lower 8K of RAM
2000-7FFF	24K RAM. (2000-73FF)
8000-FFFF	Game cartridge/Upper 32 RAM (Adam Only)

Using the Super Code Module

As the Super Game Module is an add-on module one of the first considerations should be to either ensure it is physically present if your game requires it to function and/or optionally extends the capability of your title if it is present.

On start-up the Super Game Module's RAM is disabled by default so it will not interfere with the additional memory that would already be present on an Adam computer.

The following routine 1st checks whether the system is an Adam or a ColecoVision by detecting whether additional memory is already present (see function IS_ADAM).

If it is not an Adam, it then checks for the presence of the Super Game Modules AY sound processor and if it finds it the Super Game Modules memory is enabled.

The routine also saves what it detected in a single byte of RAM (MACHINE), with 0 = ColecoVision and 1 = Adam.

So, after calling this routine, Super Game Module memory is enabled if present (and not running on an Adam) and with the machine flag being set, your game can determine whether it has the extra memory available. And if the AYPSG flag being set, your game can determine whether it has the extra AY sound chip to use.

```
;==============================
; Enable SGM Memory
;==============================
ENABLE_SGM_MEMORY:
    XOR A
    LD (MACHINE),A ; By default a machine is a ColecoVision
    LD (AYPSG),A ; By default no AY PSG
    ; don't enable SGM memory if we have an Adam
    CALL IS_ADAM
    CP 1
    JP NZ,.notAdam
    LD (MACHINE),A
.notAdam:
    ; look for the SGM PSG
    CALL PSG_TST
    CP 1
    RET NZ
    LD A,1
    LD (AYPSG),A
    ; enable SGM memory
    LD A,00000001bh
    OUT(53h),A
    RET


;==============================
; The presence of RAM between 2000h-5FFFh on boot means we have an Adam
; A = 1 if an Adam, 0 otherwise
;==============================
IS_ADAM:
    ; check for Ram at 2000h-5FFFh
    ; write values to 2000h-20FFh
    LD HL,02000h
    LD B,0FFh
ISA1:
    LD (HL),B
    INC HL
    DJNZ ISA1
    ; now read values back
    LD HL,02000h
    LD B,0FFh
ISA2:
    LD A,(HL)
    CP B
    JP Z, ISA3
    ; not a match so probably ROM
    XOR A
    RET
ISA3:
    INC HL
    DJNZ ISA2
    LD A,1
    LD (MACHINE),A ; for the moment make this machine an Adam
    RET


;==============================
; SGM PSG Ports
;==============================
PSGCTR: EQU 050h
```

```
PSGWRT:  EQU  051h
PSGRD:   EQU  052h

;==============================
; Check for the existence of a SGM PSG
; A = 1 if found, false otherwise
;==============================
PSG_TST:
    LD HL,5502H
    LD DE,0AA00H
    CALL PSG_SET
    EX DE,HL                ;5502H
    CALL PSG_SET
    EX DE,HL                ;AA00H
    CALL PSG_TST1           ;TEST BYTE
    EX DE,HL                ;5502H
    CALL PSG_TST1           ;TEST BYTE
PSG_TST3:
    ; PSG Found
    LD A,1
    RET

;1st PSG Test
PSG_TST1:
    LD A,E
    OUT (PSGCTR),A
    LD D,D
    IN A,(PSGRD)            ;READ BACK
    CP D
    RET Z                   ;RETURN IF OK
    ;IF PSG NOT FOUND
    POP DE ; Remove return point
    XOR A
    RET

;==============================
; SET SGM PSG
;==============================
PSG_SET:
    LD A,E
    OUT (PSGCTR),A          ;SET PSG REG #0
    LD A,D
    OUT (PSGWRT),A
    RET
```

References

Several documents and websites were used in compiling the technical sections of this book as follows:

References

ColecoVision Coding Guide with Absolute BIOS Listing

By Amy Purple, July 28th 2005

ColecoVision MegaCart FAQ Version 1.02

By OPCODE Games, September 7th 2013

ADAM E.O.S. Programmer's Manual

By Guy Cousineau

Smooth Criminal OS 7 Sound Demo

By Amy Purple, March 4th 2009

Image Sources

37By Evan-Amos - Own work, Public Domain, https://commons.wikimedia.org/w/index.php?curid=11421149

Index

_CHECK_FCB, 232

_CLOSE_FILE, 235

_CONS_DISP, 227

_CONS_INIT, 226

_CONS_OUT, 226

_END_PR_BUFF, 230

_END_PR_CH, 231

_END_RD_1_BLOCK, 239

_END_RD_CH_DEV, 228

_END_RD_KBD, 229

_END_WR_1_BLOCK, 240

_END_WR_CH_DEV, 230

_EOS_START, 222

_FIND_DCB, 222

_FMGR_INIT, 237

_GET_DATE, 232

_GET_DCB_ADDR, 222

_GET_PCB_ADDR, 223

_HARD_INIT, 223

_HARD_RESET_NET, 223

_INIT_TAPE_DIR, 235

_MAKE_FILE, 234

_MODE_CHECK, 233

_OPEN_FILE, 234

_PR_BUFF, 229

_PR_CH, 229

_QUERY_FILE, 233

_RD_1_BLOCK, 238

_RD_DEV_DEP_STA, 227

_RD_KBD, 228

_READ_FILE, 236

_RELOC_PCB, 224

_REQ_KBD_STAT, 227

_REQ_PR_STAT, 227

_REQ_TAPE_STAT, 239

_REQUEST_STATUS, 224

_RESET_FILE, 236

_SCAN_ACTIVE, 224

_SCAN_FOR_FILE, 237

_SET_DATE, 232

_SET_FILE, 234

_SOFT_INIT, 224

_START_PR_BUFF, 230

_START_PR_CH, 230

_START_RD_1_BLOCK, 239

_START_RD_CH_DEV, 228

_START_RD_KBD, 228

_START_WR_1_BLOCK, 240

_START_WR_CH_DEV, 229

_SYNC, 225

_TRIM_FILE, 237

_WR_1_BLOCK, 239

_WR_CH_DEV, 229

_WRITE_FILE, 236

ACTIVATE, 177

ARM_DBNCE, 197

BOOT_UP, 213

CALC_OFFSET, 178

CONT_READ, 198

CONTROLLER_INIT, 199

CONTROLLER_SCAN, 200

DECLSN, 214

DECMSN, 215

DECODER, 201

DISPLAY_LOGO, 216

ENLARGE, 208

FILL_VRAM, 163

FIRE_DBNCE, 202

FREE_SIGNAL, 191

GAME_OPT, 164

GET_BKGRND, 179

GET_VRAM, 165

INIT_SPR_ORDER, 166

INIT_TABLE, 167

INIT_TIMER, 192

INIT_WRITER, 180

JOY_DBNCE, 203

KBD_DBNCE, 204

LOAD_ASCII, 168

MODE_1, 169

MSNTOLSN, 217

PLAY_IT, 160

PLAY_SONGS, 161

POLLER, 205

PORT_COLLECTION, 223

POWER_UP, 218

PUT_FRAME, 182

PUT_VRAM, 170

PUT0SPRITE, 186

PUTCOMPLEX, 181

PUTOBJ, 184

PUTSEMI, 185

PX_TO_PTRN_POS, 187

RAND_GEN, 219

READ_REGISTER, 171

READ_VRAM, 172

REFLECT_HORZONTAL, 209

REFLECT_VERTICAL, 210

REQUEST_SIGNAL, 193

ROTATE_90, 211

SOUND_INIT, 159

SOUND_MAN, 162

TEST_SIGNAL, 194

TIME_MGR, 195

Timer Data Structures, 190

TURN_OFF_SOUND, 158

UPDATE_SPINNER, 206

WR_SPR_NM_TBL, 175

WRITE_REGISTER, 173

WRITE_VRAM, 174

www.ingramcontent.com/pod-product-compliance
Lightning Source LLC
Chambersburg PA
CBHW071239050326
40690CB00011B/2179